VIRGINIA WOOLF
1882–1941

VIRGINIA WOOLF

Her Art as a Novelist

BY

JOAN BENNETT

Fellow of Girton College, Cambridge

Second Edition

CAMBRIDGE UNIVERSITY PRESS

Published by the Syndics of the Cambridge University Press
Bentley House, 200 Euston Road, London NW1 2DB
American Branch: 32 East 57th Street, New York, N.Y. 10022

ISBNS:
0 521 04160 0 hard covers
0 521 09951 x paperback

First published 1945
Reprinted 1945, 1949
Second edition and first paperback edition 1964
Reprinted and paperback reissued 1975

First printed in Great Britain at the
University Printing House, Cambridge
Reprinted in Great Britain by
Alden & Mowbray Ltd at the Alden Press, Oxford

CONTENTS

PREFATORY NOTE AND DEDICATION

TO

GEORGE RYLANDS

I have dedicated this book to you because without your penetrating and constructive criticism it would never have been completed. But you are not to blame for its inadequacy. I have omitted what you constantly demanded, a chapter on the author's style. This book is about Virginia Woolf's vision of human life, and it is about her sense of values, and it attempts to analyse the form of her novels; but nowhere does it analyse the evocative images and flexible rhythms upon which all this depends. Yet almost every sentence bears her hall-mark. Who but she could have written:

"How fresh, how calm, stiller than this of course, the air was in the early morning; like the flap of a wave; chill and sharp and yet (for a girl of eighteen as she then was) solemn, feeling as she did, standing there at the open window, that something awful was about to happen; looking at the flowers, at the trees with the smoke winding off them and the rooks rising, falling; standing and looking until Peter Walsh said, 'Musing among the vegetables?'—was that it?— 'I prefer men to cauliflowers'—was that it?"

Her sentences feel their way from point to point, they are fluid, superficially inconsequent, yet beautifully ordered and controlled in their rhythm and their sequence of images. All this and much more the discerning reader will discover in the many quotations. Similarly he will discover her all-pervasive humour. Again and again I have quoted passages to illustrate this or that and quoted them with an apparent disregard for the play of fancy, the ironic inflections, the odd juxtapositions which are a continual source of delight. Her humour is too subtle for me to analyse; it is a sense of the incongruous, a trick of "associating things apparently unlike", a power of standing aloof and amused and yet compassionate.

Incomplete though it is, I have dedicated this book to you because it is owing to your belief that I could write it, and to the keen discernment of your criticism of my first attempts, that it is now as good as I can make it.

JOAN BENNETT

1944

PREFACE TO THE SECOND EDITION

A new edition has given me the opportunity to add two new chapters, taking account of posthumous publications, one about *A Writer's Diary* and one about Virginia Woolf's critical essays. The *Diary* enables us to watch the development of each of her novels from its first conception to its completion; this does not of course affect our response to the finished works, that will depend neither on her first intention, nor on the ensuing modification, but solely on the final result. What we can gain from the *Diary* is insight into her creative process and a fuller understanding of the technical problems that she had to solve in her continually renewed experiment in the art of fiction. Her critical essays are relevant to her art as a novelist, not only because many of them are about novels and novelists, but because her highly individual way of responding to experience is as evident in them as in her fiction. I have made no change of substance in chapters I to VI, although the modern reader probably needs less explanation of Virginia Woolf's departures from tradition than did readers in 1945. At that time it seemed proper to emphasize her innovations; today I should want to emphasize the continuity with tradition. Fiction for Virginia Woolf, as for Jane Austen or George Eliot, was a representation of life; she never used a character as a symbol nor shaped a story as an allegory. I hope the two new chapters will help to correct any over-emphasis on what she rejected and help to indicate the importance of what she retained.

1963   J.B.

THE NOVELS

OTHER WORKS

POSTHUMOUSLY PUBLISHED

All these were published by the Hogarth Press and it is owing to the kindness of Mr Leonard Woolf that I have been able to quote from them so liberally in this book.

CHAPTER I

INTRODUCTORY

In an article on *Robinson Crusoe* in *The Common Reader: Second Series*, Virginia Woolf wrote about the reader and the writer of fiction:

"Our first task, and it is often formidable enough, is to master his perspective. Until we know how the novelist orders his world, the ornaments of that world, which the critics press upon us, the adventures of the writer, to which biographers draw attention, are superfluous possessions of which we can make no use."

and Terence Hewet, in *The Voyage Out*, talking to Rachel about his as yet unwritten novels, looks at her "almost severely" and says:

"'Nobody cares. All you read a novel for is to see what sort of person the writer is, and, if you know him, which of his friends he's put in. As for the novel itself, the whole conception, the way one's seen the thing, felt about it, made it stand in relation to other things, not one in a million cares for that.'"

Although the task is "formidable", this little book is an attempt to discover from Virginia Woolf's own novels her "perspective," how she "orders her world", how she sees and feels and composes. In the same volume of essays, writing this time of Meredith, she says:

"Since the first novel is always apt to be an unguarded one, where the author displays his gifts without knowing how to dispose of them to the best advantage, we may do well to open *Richard Feverel* first." [*The Common Reader: Second Series*]

Her own first novel, *The Voyage Out* (1915), hardly seems to bear out the generalization; it is not "unguarded" in this sense, since it leaves the impression of an accomplished purpose. In

Night and Day (1919), which is in some ways richer and more ambitious and in others less satisfying than her first book, the reader has a more immediate sense of gifts not disposed of to the best advantage. But in the light of what was to follow it becomes clear that in neither novel had she wholly found herself. It is not until after the first two novels that we can say, as she says of Meredith's first, that the writer

"has been . . . at great pains to destroy the conventional form of the novel . . . ; he has destroyed all the usual staircases by which we have learnt to climb."

[*The Common Reader: Second Series*]

And yet she, no less than Meredith, needed to do this, and partly for similar reasons:

"For what reason, then, has he sacrificed the substantial advantages of realistic common sense—the staircase and the stucco? Because, it becomes clear as we read, he possessed a keen sense not of the complexity of character, but of the splendour of a scene. One after another in this first book he creates a scene to which we can attach abstract names—Youth, The Birth of Love, The Power of Nature. . . . We forget that Richard is Richard and that Lucy is Lucy; they are youth; the world runs molten gold. The writer is a rhapsodist, a poet then; but we have not yet exhausted all the elements in this first novel. . . . The book is cracked through and through with those fissures which come when the author seems to be of twenty minds at the same time. Yet it succeeds in holding miraculously together, not certainly by the depths and originality of its character drawing but by the vigour of its intellectual power and by its lyrical intensity."

[*The Common Reader: Second Series*]

There are immense differences between Virginia Woolf's vision of life and Meredith's; but in the lyricism to which she points there is a similarity, and it will cause her to destroy the mould of the traditional novel as he did and to create a form more remote from traditional prose fiction than any he invented.

2

In the meanwhile, in her first two books, she takes the basic principles of the novel as she finds them and adapts them to her own vision. Characters are described and then gradually made better known to us by their sayings and doings; they are related to one another by a series of events leading to a climax. Each book is a love story. Yet it is clear that it is not the width and variety of the human comedy, nor the idiosyncrasies of human character, that most interest her. Rather it is the deep and simple human experiences, love, happiness, beauty, loneliness, death. Again and again in these two books what the reader feels is not so much "this man or woman would have felt like that in those circumstances," but rather "Yes, that is how it feels to be in love; to be happy; to be desolate".

"'We don't care for people because of their qualities,' he tried to explain. 'It's just them we care for,'—he struck a match—'just that,' he said, pointing to the flames." [*The Voyage Out*]

Hewet says that to Evelyn Murgatroyd at a certain moment and in a certain scene; it is perfectly appropriate to the circumstances and to the characters; but it transcends them:

"She realized with a great sense of comfort how easily she could talk to Hewet, those thorns or ragged corners which tear the surface of some relationships being smoothed away." [*The Voyage Out*]

It is Rachel who has this experience; but what it reveals is not her character, it is an aspect of love:

"Very gently and quietly, almost as if it were the blood singing in her veins, or the water of the stream running over stones, Rachel became conscious of a new feeling within her. She wondered for a moment what it was, and then said to herself, with a little surprise at recognizing in her own person so famous a thing:

3

"'This is happiness, I suppose.' And aloud to Terence she spoke, 'This is happiness.'

"On the heels of her words he answered, 'This is happiness', upon which they guessed that the feeling had sprung in both of them at the same time." [*The Voyage Out*]

Night and Day, with its more complex story and its wider social scene, has at the heart of it this same preoccupation with the universal nature of love and happiness. Mary Datchet and Ralph Denham are walking together fiercely arguing about government, law, the social structure:

"At length they drew breath, let the argument fly into the limbo of other good arguments, and, leaning over a gate, opened their eyes for the first time and looked about them. Their feet tingled with warm blood and their breath rose in steam about them. The bodily exercise made them both feel more direct and less self-conscious than usual, and Mary, indeed, was overcome by a sort of light-headedness which made it seem to her that it mattered very little what happened next. It mattered so little, indeed, that she felt herself on the point of saying to Ralph: 'I love you; I shall never love anybody else. Marry me or leave me—I don't care a straw.' At the moment, however, speech or silence seemed immaterial, and she merely clapped her hands together, and looked at the distant woods with the rust-like bloom on their brown, and the green and blue landscape through the steam of her own breath. It seemed a mere toss up whether she said, 'I love you', or whether she said, 'I love the beech trees', or only 'I love—I love'." [*Night and Day*]

The reader knows Mary Datchet well, and at many points in the book it is her individual character that emerges from her action or her words; but here it is youth and love itself, the fundamental and simple experience of which poets write. Katharine Hilbery and Ralph Denham, on the other hand, are not wholly clear to the reader as individuals even at the end of the book. The idiosyncrasies that differentiate them from other people are unimportant—when we think of them from this point of view they appear a little misty; what we remember about them are those vivid experiences through which they become conscious of the bonds that unite them. Ralph meets Katharine in the street by chance:

"Thus it came about that he saw Katharine Hilbery coming towards him and looked straight at her, as if she was only an illustration of the argument that was going forward in his mind. In this spirit he noticed the rather set expression in her eyes, and the slight, half-conscious movement of her lips, which, together with her height and the distinction of her dress, made her look as if the scurrying crowd impeded her, and her direction were different from theirs. He noticed this calmly; but suddenly, as he passed her, his hands and knees began to tremble, and his heart beat painfully. She did not see him, and went on repeating to herself some lines which had stuck in her memory: 'It's life that matters, nothing but life—the process of discovering—the everlasting and perpetual process, not the discovery itself at all.' Thus occupied, she did not see Denham, and he had not the courage to stop her. But immediately the whole scene in the Strand wore that curious look of order and purpose which is imparted to the most heterogeneous things when music sounds, and so pleasant was this impression that he was very glad that he had not stopped her, after all. It grew slowly fainter, but lasted until he stood outside the barrister's chambers."

[*Night and Day*]

It is not Ralph and Katharine as individuals that matters here but the experience unveiled in their encounter. Similarly, in the way of the poets and of certain novelists who were also poets, Emily Brontë or Meredith or Hardy, Virginia Woolf evokes in each of these first two books scenes that communicate what it felt like to be young. At certain moments in *Night and Day* Cassandra is not so much Cassandra as youth itself:

"To Cassandra's ears the buzz of voices inside the drawing-room was like the tuning up of the instruments of the orchestra. It seemed to her that there were numbers of people in the room, and that they were strangers, and that they were beautiful and dressed with the greatest distinction, although they proved to be mostly her relations, and the distinction of their clothing was confined, in the eyes of an impartial observer, to the white waistcoat which Rodney wore. But they all rose simultaneously, which was by itself impressive, and they all exclaimed, and shook hands, and she was introduced to Mr Peyton, and the door sprang open, and dinner was announced, and they filed off, William Rodney offering her his slightly bent black arm, as she secretly hoped he would. In short, had the scene been looked at only through her eyes, it must have been described as one of magical brilliancy. The pattern of the soup plates, the stiff folds of the napkins, which rose by the side of each plate in the shape of arum lilies, the long sticks of bread tied with pink ribbon, the silver dishes and the sea-coloured champagne glasses, with the flakes of gold congealed in their stems—all these details, together with a curiously pervasive smell of kid-gloves, con-tributed to her exhilaration, which must be repressed however, because she was grown-up, and the world held no more for her to marvel at.

"The world held no more for her to marvel at, it is true; but it held other people, and each other person possessed in Cas-sandra's mind some fragment of what privately she called 'reality'. It was a gift that they would impart if you asked them for it, and thus no dinner party could possibly be dull, and little Mr Peyton on her right and William Rodney on her left were in equal measure endowed with the quality which seemed to her so unmistakable and so precious that the way people neglected to demand it was a constant source of surprise to her. She scarcely knew, indeed, whether she was talking to Mr Peyton or to William Rodney. But to one who, by degrees, assumed the shape of an elderly man with a moustache, she described how she had arrived in London that very afternoon, and how she had taken a cab and driven through the streets. Mr Peyton, an editor of fifty years, bowed his bald head repeatedly, with apparent understanding. At least, he understood that she was very young and pretty, and saw that she was excited, though he could not gather at once from her words or remember from his own experience what there was to be excited about. 'Were there any buds on the trees?' he asked. 'Which line did she travel by?'"

[*Night and Day*]

Rachel, in *The Voyage Out*, has the same unimpaired expectancy; she is, indeed, less of a "character" than Cassandra, less a peculiar, differentiated specimen of humanity, and her experience more constantly represents the quality of youth itself. Sitting next to Richard Dalloway at a meal on the ship:

"Rachel had other questions on the tip of her tongue; or rather one enormous question, which she did not in the least know how to put into words. The talk appeared too airy to admit of it.

"'Please tell me—everything.' That was what she wanted to say. He had drawn apart one little chink and showed astonishing treasures. It seemed to her incredible that a man like that should be willing to talk to her. He had sisters and pets and once lived in the country. She stirred her tea round and round; the bubbles which swam and clustered in the cup seemed to her like the union of their minds." [*The Voyage Out*]

And, like Cassandra, Rachel experiences the irrational excitement or intoxication of self-discovery:

"The vision of her own personality, of herself as a real everlasting thing, different from anything else, unmergeable, like the sea or the wind, flashed into Rachel's mind, and she became profoundly excited at the thought of living." [*The Voyage Out*]

In these first two books the moments which remain most memorable are those in which we become aware of those deeper levels of experience where human beings are alike, rather than of the inexhaustible variety of human character. In the profoundly moving scenes at the end of *The Voyage Out*, what we know about Terence or Rachel or Helen or Hirst as individuals matters little compared with our sense of the capacity for suffering they have in common with ourselves. Because, in *The Voyage Out*, the characters are removed from the common-place world of everyday duties and pleasures, on the ship and then on the island, this lyrical content is less interrupted. The book, though in some ways narrower than *Night and Day* and less rich in promise, is more successfully integrated.

The traditional, story-telling form of the novel allows scope for those moments of heightened consciousness in which superficial differences of character are submerged beneath the tide of feeling. But it is not only in these lyrical scenes that Virginia Woolf's individual perspective is manifest in her first two novels. Beside these moments of heightened consciousness are other human experiences of which she has a peculiar understanding. In her later books, indeed, romantic, passionate love is seldom in the foreground. She is more frequently occupied with the fruit that sometimes ripens from that seed, the relation between friends or between husband and wife. It is shown here in the relations between Mr and Mrs Dalloway, between Mr and Mrs Ambrose or between Mr and Mrs Hilbery; between each pair there is a community of mind which does not require speech or explanation:

"They both laughed, thinking the same things, so that there was no need to compare their impressions." [*The Voyage Out*]

That is Mr and Mrs Dalloway, alone together after their first encounter with the Ambroses and the Vinraces. Or the writer introduces a scene between Mr and Mrs Ambrose:

"When two people have been married for years they seem to become unconscious of each other's bodily presence so that they

8

move as if alone, speak aloud things which they do not expect to be answered, and in general seem to experience all the comfort of solitude without its loneliness." [*The Voyage Out*]

Terence Hewet has observed this secret understanding between married people, and, when he discovers that his feeling for Rachel is love, he recoils from its consequences because he has resented the exclusiveness of married love:

"He instantly decided that he did not want to marry any one. Partly because he was irritated by Rachel the idea of marriage irritated him. It immediately suggested the picture of two people sitting alone over the fire; the man was reading, the woman sewing. There was a second picture. He saw a man jump up, say good night, leave the company and hasten away with the quiet secret look of one who is stealing to certain happiness. Both these pictures were very unpleasant, and even more so was a third picture, of husband and wife and friend; and the married people glancing at each other as though they were content to let something pass unquestioned, being themselves possessed of the deeper truth." [*The Voyage Out*]

The later books show much more fully the gradual development of such relationships and the art of living whereby they are created. But the genius of Mrs Ramsay (*To the Lighthouse*) is foreshadowed in certain scenes where Clarissa disposes of the physical discomforts that irritate Richard when he first comes on board ship; or where Helen soothes and mocks Ridley's scholarly vanity; or where Mrs Hilbery, deliciously vague and inconsequent though she is, unravels the tangles that have accumulated round her husband in her absence. The continuity of love, its ebb and flow through a lifetime, will be a more frequent theme in the later novels than the moments of crisis; in the long run affection and devotion interest Virginia Woolf more than passion.

It is discernible, even in these first two novels, that what Virginia Woolf most clearly perceives, is what the experience of living feels like to the people she creates. Inevitably that will depend upon their circumstances, upon the time, the place, the position in an economic and social structure in which they find themselves. The moral, social, economic and religious problems which play so large a part in the novels of the nineteenth century are important in her books too, but we are made aware of them only as they colour the world for the people she presents and form part of what life feels like to them. At the beginning of *The Voyage Out*, before England is left behind we are shown the effect of some of them upon the mind of Helen Ambrose:

"She knew how to read the people who were passing her; there were the rich who were running to and from each other's houses at this hour; there were the bigoted workers driving in a straight line to their offices; there were the poor who were unhappy and rightly malignant. Already, though there was sunlight in the haze, tattered old men and women were nodding off to sleep upon the seats. When one gave up seeing the beauty that clothed things, this was the skeleton beneath." [*The Voyage Out*]

Social and economic conditions affect the Dalloways in a different fashion. They represent a type whose way of living is contrasted with the more contemplative way of scholars or artists represented by the Ambroses and their friends—people who translate Pindar, or read philosophy, enjoy music, or write poetry. In their circle Richard Dalloway feels a need to justify himself:

"'We politicians doubtless seem to you' (he grasped somehow that Helen was representative of the arts) 'a gross commonplace set of people; but we see both sides, we may be clumsy, but we do our best to get a grasp of things. Now your artists find things in a mess, shrug their shoulders, turn aside to their visions—which I grant may be very beautiful—and leave things in a mess. Now that seems to me evading one's responsibilities. Besides we aren't all born with the artistic faculty.'" [*The Voyage Out*]

On the island it is mainly Evelyn Murgatroyd who represents this opposition of the active to the contemplative nature, with her desire to embrace causes and to form societies for putting down this and that:

"'So what I'm going to tell 'em is that we've talked enough about art, and we'd better begin to talk about life for a change. Questions that really matter to people's lives, the White Slave Traffic, Women's Suffrage, The Insurance Bill and so on.'" [*The Voyage Out*]

But, because the scene is remote from England, this life of action is only reflected in the minds of the characters; it is what Richard or Evelyn think and feel about what they have done, or will do; what we actually see them doing is living a life bounded by personal relations. In *Night and Day*, where the story is set in England, different groups of characters live the life of action or of contemplation. Around Mary Datchet moves the circle of those who try to ameliorate the social structure; while around Katharine Hilbery moves the circle of poets, scholars, philosophers, or women whose art is the art of civilized living. Moreover, on this wider canvas, the author paints the scene itself, not only its effect in consciousness; the cultured and elegant home of the Hilberys contrasted with the genteel poverty of the Denhams; the overcrowded town house of the Denhams contrasted with Mary Datchet's rural vicarage home. The reader's attention is divided between this diversity of environment and of endeavour, which illustrates certain aspects of modern life and the other, deeper theme, the life experience of five people whose interrelations make up the pattern of the story.

Night and Day was published in 1919. In the same year Virginia Woolf wrote an essay on contemporary fiction, which is now in *The Common Reader: First Series*. In it she expresses her dissatisfaction with the current form of the novel as represented by the novels of Arnold Bennett:

"Can it be that, owing to one of those little deviations which the human spirit seems to make from time to time, Mr Bennett has come down with his magnificent apparatus for catching life just an inch or two on the wrong side? Life escapes; and perhaps without life nothing else is worth while. It is a confession of vagueness to have to make use of such a figure as this; but we scarcely better the matter by speaking, as critics are prone to do, of reality. Admitting the vagueness which afflicts all criticism of novels, let us hazard the opinion that for us at this moment the form of fiction most in vogue more often misses than secures the thing we seek. Whether we call it life or spirit, truth or reality, this, the essential thing, has moved off, or on, and refuses to be contained any longer in such ill fitting vestments as we provide. Nevertheless we go on perseveringly, conscientiously, constructing our two and thirty chapters after a design which more and more ceases to resemble the vision in our minds."

[The Common Reader: First Series]

The novelist designs his book to present life as he sees and understands it. The convention of plot and interrelated character is a means of imposing order on the flux and chaos of experience. Order and relation may or may not exist elsewhere, but they undoubtedly exist in the mind of man and to our minds "truth is stranger than fiction", because in fiction an order has been imposed on, or elicited from, experience by the writer. The form of the novel which prevailed in the first quarter of this century seemed to Virginia Woolf to obscure or even to falsify her experience. But for every form that is defied, new forms or conventions arise, because the human mind is so constituted that it cannot deal with chaos, it sees only what is selected or arranged. Virginia Woolf set herself to destroy the current form of the novel and was then driven to invent one which would express her own vision of life. Some aspects of that vision, which conflicted with the so-called realistic novel, are indicated in her essay:

"Look within and life, it seems, is very far from being 'like this'. Examine for a moment an ordinary mind on an ordinary day. The mind receives a myriad impressions—trivial, fantastic, evanescent, or engraved with the sharpness of steel. From all sides they come, an incessant shower of innumerable atoms; and as they fall, as they shape themselves into the life of Monday or Tuesday, the accent falls differently from of old; the moment of importance came not here but there; so that, if the writer were a free man and not a slave, if he could write what he chose, not what he must, if he could base his work upon his own feeling and not upon convention, there would be no plot, no comedy, no tragedy, no love interest or catastrophe in the accepted style.... Life is not a series of gig lamps symmetrically arranged; life is a luminous halo, a semi transparent envelope surrounding us from the beginning of consciousness to the end. Is it not the task of the novelist to convey this varying, this unknown and uncircumscribed spirit, whatever aberration or complexity it may display....?" [*The Common Reader: First Series*]

In a sense, of course, the answer is "no it is not", and Virginia Woolf was far too great an artist not to discover this. All art implies selection, arrangement, order, and therefore conventions. She is pushing her problem to an extreme; it is, nevertheless, a vital problem; out of her solution to it will come her own peculiar and significant contribution to the art of the novel. By 1919, when this essay on contemporary fiction was published, others, both in France and in England, had felt a similar dissatisfaction with what may be called "the Arnold Bennett form". Dorothy M. Richardson published the first volume of *Pilgrimage* in 1915; in the foreword to the 1938 edition[1] she describes how, believing herself to be a lonely explorer, she discovered that she was in fact one of a company:

"In 1913, the opening pages of the attempted chronicle became the first chapter of *Pilgrimage*, written to the accompaniment of

1 J. M. Dent and Sons, Ltd. and the Cresset Press.

a sense of being upon a fresh pathway, an adventure so searching and, sometimes, so joyous as to produce a longing for participation;...In 1915, the covering title being at the moment in use elsewhere, it was published as *Pointed Roofs*.

"The lonely track, meanwhile, had turned out to be a populous highway...."

She refers to Gertrude Stein and to James Joyce, who had by this time published only *Dubliners*, and continues:

"News came from France of one Marcel Proust, said to be producing an unprecedentedly profound and opulent reconstruction of experience focused from within the mind of a single individual, and, since Proust's first volume had been published and several others written by 1913, the France of Balzac now seemed to have produced the earliest adventurer.

"Finally, however, the role of pathfinder was declared to have been played by a venerable gentleman, a charmed and charming high priest of nearly all the orthodoxies, inhabiting a softly lit enclosure he mistook, until 1914, for the universe....

"And while, indeed, it is possible to claim for Henry James, keeping the reader incessantly watching the conflict of human forces through the eye of a single observer, rather than taking him, before the drama begins, upon a tour amongst the properties, or breaking in with descriptive introductions of the players as one by one they enter his enclosed resounding chamber, where no plant grows and no mystery pours in from the unheeded stars, a far from inconsiderable technical influence, it was nevertheless not without a sense of relief that the present writer recently discovered, in *Wilhelm Meister*, the following manifesto:

"'In the novel, reflections and incidents should be featured; in drama character and action. The novel must proceed slowly, and the thought processes of the principal figure must, by one device or another, hold up the development of the whole....The hero of the novel must be acted upon, or, at any rate, not himself the principal operator....Grandison, Clarissa, Pamela, The Vicar of Wakefield, and Tom Jones himself, even where they are not acted upon, are still retarding personalities and all the incidents are, in a certain measure, modelled according to their thoughts.'"

[*Pilgrimage*, by Dorothy Richardson]

She does not state why she was relieved, we are left to infer the reasons. It was, no doubt, partly because the passage from *Wilhelm Meister* implied that her own work was in the main tradition of the novel. It was also, apparently, distasteful to her to be too closely related to Henry James, not perhaps so much because in his world "no plant grows and no mystery pours from the unheeded stars", for that is equally true of Richardson's world, but because James's extreme concern with form was alien to her. Her own volumes record the experience of Miriam with delicate precision but with hardly more selection or arrangement than memory would provide.

All experience implies a degree of selection, even prior to the involuntary omissions caused by oblivion. The normal man, as distinct from the artist, selects in the act of becoming conscious of his experience. This, I take it, is what Coleridge, deriving his conception from Kant, meant by "the primary imagination". Professor D. G. James explains this with admirable clarity in his wise and illuminating book, *Scepticism and Poetry*:

"The activity of the mind is synthetic of what is given, and is creative in the sense that the world is not given as an ordered unity to the mind, and that the mind is not a mirror in which the world is reflected or a blank sheet upon which the world imprints itself. Instead the mind actively grasps and operates upon what is presented in sensation."

Form then, in this elementary sense, is a condition of experience, the selecting and ordering of this "primary imagination" is involuntary; because the mind cannot cope with a chaotic multiplicity of sensations, it gives hospitality only to an ordered and limited number of them. *Pilgrimage* has form in this sense;

it has the effect of autobiography written by one who is exceptionally perceptive and knows how to define in words the quality of her experience. But form as Henry James understood it is a product of the "secondary imagination" which, Coleridge writes:

"I consider as an echo of the former" (the primary) "co-existing with the conscious will, yet still as identical with the primary in the kind of its agency, and differing only in degree and in the mode of its operation. It dissolves, diffuses, dissipates, in order to recreate...." [*Biographia Literaria* c. XIII]

When Virginia Woolf discovered that life, as she saw it, and therefore her subject as a novelist, was "what the mind receives on an ordinary day", two courses were open to her. That she must reject the current form as represented in the works of Arnold Bennett or of Galsworthy was clear. But should she content herself with recording impressions as they flow in upon the mind or should she invite her "secondary imagination" to "recreate" by eliciting an order from those impressions? There were two principal reasons, I believe, why she chose the latter course. In the first place her genius was not autobiographical, she was not preponderantly interested in herself, so that she could not be satisfied with recording only the direct impressions made upon her own mind. This is implied in some of the things she says about the early work of James Joyce, in the essay already referred to:

"Let us record the atoms as they fall upon the mind in the order in which they fall, let us trace the pattern, however disconnected and incoherent in appearance, which each sight or incident scores upon the consciousness. Let us not take it for granted that life exists more fully in what is commonly thought big than in what is commonly thought small. Any one who has read *The Portrait of the Artist as a Young Man* or, what promises to be a far more interesting work, *Ulysses*, now appearing in the *Little Review*, will have hazarded some theory of this nature as to Mr Joyce's intention. On our part, with such a fragment before us, it is hazarded rather than affirmed; but whatever the intention of the whole, there can be no question but that it is of the utmost sincerity and that the result, difficult or unpleasant as we may judge it, is undeniably important....Mr Joyce...is concerned at all costs to reveal the flickerings of that innermost flame which flashes its messages through the brain, and in order to preserve it he disregards with complete courage whatever seems to him adventitious, whether it be probability, or coherence, or any other of those signposts which for generations have served to support the imagination of a reader when called upon to imagine what he can neither touch nor see....If we want life itself, here surely we have it."   [*The Common Reader: First Series*]

But when she has thus paid homage, she speaks of misgivings, and her misgivings are no less revealing of her own purposes as a writer than is her appreciation:

"Is it the method that inhibits the creative power? Is it due to the method that we feel neither jovial nor magnanimous, but centred in a self which, in spite of its tremor of susceptibility, never embraces or creates what is outside itself and beyond?"

The intricate and disciplined form of her own best novels is a means of escaping from a single point of view and creating "what is outside and beyond". Form enables her in *To the Lighthouse*, *Mrs Dalloway*, *The Waves* and *Between the Acts* to move from mind to mind without confusion, to present diversity of experience within a single design. To do this she needed her subtle handling of sequences, her skilful juxtapositions and transitions, composing a formal whole. But it is not only because she is not content with autobiography that she elicits a pattern from her vision of life. Another reason is suggested in part of a conversation between Hewet and Rachel in *The Voyage Out*:

"'What I want to do in writing novels is very much what you want to do when you play the piano, I expect', he began, turning and speaking over his shoulder. 'We want to find out what's behind things, don't we?—Look at the lights down there', he continued, 'scattered about anyhow. Things I feel come to me like lights....I want to combine them....Have you ever seen fireworks that make figures?...I want to make figures.... Is that what you want to do?'

"Now they were out on the road and could walk side by side.

"'When I play the piano? Music is different....But I see what you mean.' They tried to invent theories and to make their theories agree. As Hewet had no knowledge of music, Rachel took his stick and drew figures in the thin white dust to explain how Bach wrote his fugues."

[*The Voyage Out*]

Like Hewet, she wants "to find out what's behind things", and for her, as for him, this desire is expressed in an endeavour "to combine...to make figures". Her novels are penetrated through and through with a sense of the strangeness of human life, as though there were some other life guessed at, more ordered and significant, of which men catch an occasional glimpse. She needed to express her own peculiar feeling about these islands of time in which we live surrounded by the great ocean of historic and prehistoric time, and her own nostalgia for those indefinable abstractions, Beauty and Truth; to do this she was impelled to invent for the novel a form akin to poetic form.

CHAPTER II

CHARACTERS AND HUMAN BEINGS

Mr E. M. Forster[1] writes of Virginia Woolf

"she could seldom so portray a character that it was remembered afterwards on its own account, as Emma is remembered, for instance, or Dorothea Casaubon, or Sophia and Constance in *The Old Wives' Tale*."

Nor is Mr Forster alone in feeling that Virginia Woolf's mature novels fail to provide a gallery of memorable portraits, such as can be derived from the works of other great novelists. However that may be, it is certain that she developed a different method of characterization from theirs, and one that produces a different effect. In her first two books some, but not all, of the characters are first introduced in the traditional way. Mr Hilbery, who plays a minor role in *Night and Day*, is sketched for the reader at his first appearance:

"He was an elderly man, with a pair of oval, hazel eyes which were rather bright for his time of life, and relieved the heaviness of his face. He played constantly with a little green stone attached to his watch chain, thus displaying long and very sensitive fingers, and had a habit of moving his head hither and thither very quickly without altering the position of his large and rather corpulent body, so that he seemed to be providing himself incessantly with food for amusement and reflection with the least possible expenditure of energy. One might suppose that he had passed the time of life when his ambitions were personal, or that he had gratified them as far as he was likely to do, and now employed his considerable acuteness rather to observe and reflect than to attain any result."   [*Night and Day*]

1 *Virginia Woolf*, by E. M. Forster, Cambridge University Press, 1942.

The fault here is a slight overloading with detail, and the physical traits are made to carry an undue burden of psychological significance, a common fault with this type of presentation. The essential characteristics of an outline portrait are there, the key to the character is given, Mr Hilbery is an individual not merely a type, his main characteristics are easily remembered and can be developed and confirmed by his subsequent behaviour, thus giving the reader the self-gratulatory feeling of having understood him from the first. Mary Datchet, a more important character in the book, the complement of the more elusive heroine, Katharine Hilbery, is introduced by the same method:

"She was some twenty-five years of age, but looked older because she earned, or intended to earn, her own living, and had already lost the look of the irresponsible spectator and taken on that of the private in the army of workers. Her gestures seemed to have a certain purpose; the muscles round eyes and lips were set rather firmly, as though the senses had undergone some discipline, and were held ready for a call upon them. She had contracted two faint lines between her eyebrows, not from anxiety but from thought, and it was quite evident that all the feminine instincts of pleasing, soothing and charming were crossed by others in no way peculiar to her sex. For the rest she was brown-eyed, a little clumsy in movement, and suggested country-birth and a descent from hard-working ancestors, who had been men of faith and integrity rather than doubters or fanatics."

[*Night and Day*]

But the presentation of Rachel, in *The Voyage Out*, and of Katharine Hilbery, in *Night and Day*, is of a different kind; the reader discovers them gradually, and incompletely, in part from their own speech and reflections, in part from their effect upon other people. They are more elusive than Mr Hilbery or Mary Datchet, just as, in real life, the people we know intimately are more elusive than our acquaintance—we are aware that there is always something more to be discovered. The first picture we have of Rachel is a picture in the mind of Helen Ambrose:

"Helen looked at her. Her face was weak rather than decided, saved from insipidity by the large enquiring eyes; denied beauty, now that she was sheltered indoors, by the lack of colour and definite outline. Moreover, a hesitation in speaking, or rather a tendency to use the wrong words, made her seem more than normally incompetent for her years. Mrs Ambrose, who had been speaking much at random, now reflected that she certainly did not look forward to the intimacy of three or four weeks on board ship which was threatened. Women of her own age usually boring her, she supposed that girls would be worse. She glanced at Rachel again. Yes! how clear it was that she would be vacillating, emotional, and when you said something to her it would make no more lasting impression than the stroke of a stick upon water. There was nothing to take hold of in girls—nothing hard, permanent, satisfactory." [*The Voyage Out*]

But the book, instead of developing and confirming this impression, contradicts it at many points; Helen has not taken the place of an omniscient narrator and given the reader a clue to Rachel's character; she has revealed a little of herself and of the first impression Rachel makes on a critical observer, but no more. Katharine in *Night and Day* is introduced as Denham first sees her, and there also we are not given the illusion that the picture is complete, nor even necessarily correct. Even in these first two books the people who most interest the reader cannot be summed up. When Mary Datchet attempts to find a label for Katharine, the reader is left in no doubt of its inadequacy:

"Mary felt herself baffled, and put back again into the position in which she had been at the beginning of their talk. It seemed to her that Katharine possessed a curious power of drawing near and receding, which sent alternate emotions through her far more quickly than was usual, and kept her in a condition of curious alertness. Desiring to classify her, Mary bethought her of the convenient term 'egoist'.

"'She's an egoist', she said to herself, and stored that word up to give to Ralph one day when, as it would certainly fall out, they were discussing Miss Hilbery." [Night and Day]

The irrelevance of the classifying word is obvious both in its immediate context and in relation to the rest of our knowledge of Katharine. The word "egoist" tells us little about Katharine, but it expresses a need of Mary's, the need to define her and so be able to control her own reactions to Katharine's dynamic personality. She can only do this by holding her at a distance and so getting her as it were into focus. Virginia Woolf came to believe that all definition of character involved such a refusal to come near and that *character* in the sense in which the word is used of persons in fiction or, as often as not in biography, does not exist in real life. It is possible that the impression that she does not create clear or memorable characters is due to the fact that her portraits are of a different kind from those to which the reader of fiction is accustomed. The experience of reading fiction is analogous to the experience of looking at a painting. The painter's vision of his subject, his selection, placing and apportioning of objects or his interpretation of colour relations, are not only delightful in themselves, they also invite the beholder to see similar objects in nature in a new way, incorporating as much of the artist's vision as he has been able to assimilate. When a painter sees very differently from his predecessors, he will depart from the established conventions and, in all probability, he will paint in such a way that the majority of his public will at first be unable to discern any relation between his canvas and their own vision of the object in nature. Virginia Woolf's account of the first reception by the London public of the post-impressionist painters supplies an historical instance:

"It is difficult in 1939, when a great hospital is benefiting from a centenary exhibition of Cézanne's works, and the gallery is daily crowded with devout and submissive worshippers, to realize what violent emotions those pictures excited less than thirty years ago. The pictures are the same; it is the public that has changed. But there can be no doubt about the fact. The public in 1910 was thrown into paroxysms of rage and laughter. They went from Cézanne to Gauguin and from Gauguin to Van Gogh, they went from Picasso to Signac, and from Derain to Friesz, and they were infuriated. The pictures were a joke, and a joke at their expense. One great lady asked to have her name removed from the Committee. One gentleman, according to Desmond MacCarthy, laughed so loud at Cézanne's portrait of his wife that 'he had to be taken out and walked up and down in the fresh air for five minutes. Fine ladies went into silvery trills of laughter'. The secretary had to provide a book in which the public wrote down their complaints. Never less than four hundred people visited the gallery daily. And they expressed their opinions not only to the secretary but in letters to the director himself. The pictures were outrageous, anarchistic, and childish. They were an insult to the British public and the man who was responsible for the insult was either a fool, an impostor or a knave."

[*Roger Fry: A Biography*]

Gradually, however, a new school of painting, if it arises out of a genuine visual perception, extends the vision of the beholders and ceases to seem odd. Nature may even be thought to have been faithfully represented for the first time by the new school. This conclusion is as false as the original rejection, since "the mind is not a mirror in which the world is reflected". A great number of patterns can, with equal fidelity, be elicited from the multiple impressions offered to the eye by a single scene or one human face. Thus it is also with the serious novelist:

"since he is a single person with one sensibility the aspects of life in which he can believe with conviction are strictly limited."

[*The Common Reader: First Series*]

After 1919 the aspects of life in which Virginia Woolf could "believe with conviction" ceased to include the clearly definable human character. The people in her later books frequently express her own unwillingness to circumscribe human beings within the compass of a *character*. Mrs Dalloway, for instance:

"She would not say of anyone in the world now that they were this or that."   [*Mrs Dalloway*]

Or Mrs Ramsay, reflecting on the nature of the self:

"...one after another, she, Lily, Augustus Carmichael, must feel, our apparitions, the things you know us by, are simply childish. Beneath it is all dark, it is all spreading, it is unfathomably deep; but now and again we rise to the surface and that is what you see us by."   [*To the Lighthouse*]

Or Bernard:

"We are not simple as our friends would have us to meet their needs. Yet love is simple."   [*The Waves*]

Or Eleanor:

"These little snapshot pictures of people left much to be desired, these little surface pictures that one made, like a fly crawling over a face, and feeling, here's the nose, here's the brow."   [*The Years*]

Or Peggy Pargiter:

"I'm good, she thought, at fact collecting. But what makes up a person—(she hollowed her hand), the circumference—no, I'm not good at that."   [*The Years*]

When Virginia Woolf became fully conscious that the traditional method of characterization could not interpret her own vision of human beings, she sought for other means of communicating it. *Jacob's Room* is the first of her novels which wholly rejects the old method; but in it her new technique is not yet used with the ease and assurance she was later to acquire. Jacob Flanders is never directly described, and he rarely reveals himself to the reader by what he says or does. Instead we derive our impression of him from the effect he produces on other people in the novel, for instance, upon Mrs Norman who travels in a train to Cambridge with him:

"Nobody sees anyone as he is, let alone an elderly lady sitting opposite a strange young man in a railway carriage. They see a whole—they see all sorts of things—they see themselves.... Mrs Norman now read three pages of one of Mr Norris's novels. Should she say to the young man (and after all he was just the same age as her own boy): 'If you want to smoke, don't mind me'? No: he seemed absolutely indifferent to her presence... she did not wish to interrupt.

But since, even at her age, she noted his indifference, presumably he was in some way or other—to her at least—nice, handsome, interesting, distinguished, well built, like her own boy? One must do the best one can with her report. Anyhow, this was Jacob Flanders, aged nineteen. It is no use trying to sum people up. One must follow hints, not exactly what is said, nor yet entirely what is done...." [Jacob's Room]

This, relatively to the later novels, is a crude piece of work. It betrays uneasiness. The writer obtrudes herself in a way in which she will not do in her more mature books; by doing so she disturbs the illusion. But the foundation of the new technique is laid. The impact of one personality upon another continues in all her books to be an important means of composing the portrait of a human being. Throughout *Jacob's Room* we observe Jacob through the eyes of others:

"'I like Jacob Flanders', wrote Clara Durrant in her diary. 'He is so unworldly. He gives himself no airs, and one can say what one likes to him, though he's frightening because....'

But Mr Letts allows little space in his shilling diaries. Clara was not the one to encroach upon Wednesday. Humblest, most candid of women! 'No, no, no', she sighed, standing at the green-house door, 'don't break—don't spoil'—what? Something infinitely wonderful.

"But then, this is only a young woman's language, one, too, who loves, or refrains from loving. She wished the moment to continue for ever precisely as it was that July morning. And moments don't."

Then we are given a glimpse of what Jacob is actually doing at that moment and, to offset Clara's romantic impression, he is exchanging stories and rather coarse jokes with his male friends at an inn. There follows a series of reflections of Jacob in the minds of other people, including his mother:

"Betty Flanders was romantic about Archer and tender about John; she was unreasonably irritated by Jacob's clumsiness in the house.

"Captain Barfoot liked him best of the boys; but as for saying why....It seems then that men and women are equally at fault. It seems that a profound, impartial, and absolutely just opinion of our fellow-creatures is utterly unknown. Either we are men, or we are women. Either we are cold, or we are sentimental. Either we are young, or growing old. In any case we are but a procession of shadows, and God knows why it is that we embrace them so eagerly, and see them depart with such anguish, being shadows. And why, if this and much more is true, why are we yet surprised in the window corner by a sudden vision that the young man in the chair is of all things in the world the most real, the most solid, the best known to us—why indeed? For the moment after we know nothing about him.

"Such is the manner of our seeing. Such the conditions of our love."
[Jacob's Room]

From the conviction here expressed about the incompleteness of our knowledge of one another; and from the certainty here communicated that our fellow-beings do nevertheless arouse in us profound and valued feelings, springs Virginia Woolf's individual art of creating human beings. The method is cumulative, and it is therefore impossible to isolate from her books a portrait which epitomizes a particular character, either by means of description or dramatization. Nevertheless, it seems to me false to suggest, as Mr Forster does, that the beings she creates are less memorable than the persons in other great works of fiction. Mrs Ramsay, Mrs Dalloway, Eleanor Pargiter, each of the main personalities in *Between the Acts*, and many others from her books, inhabit the mind of the reader and enlarge the capacity for imaginative sympathy. It is sympathy rather than judgment that she invokes, her personages are apprehended rather than comprehended. Increasingly the writer eliminates herself from her books, the illusion of the all-seeing eye is replaced by the illusion that we are seeing by glimpses, with our own imperfect vision. Far more, however, is set before our eyes in the books than in normal experience. Not only are we given the impression made upon other minds, but also the impressions received and formulated by the divers persons whose lives are interwoven for us and from the pattern of the book.

In creative power Virginia Woolf can bear comparison with the great masters of prose fiction. Despite the difficulty of isolating a detail from the whole picture it is worth while to make the attempt. Even if injustice is done to the modern writer by this method it will at least serve to illustrate the difference in kind between hers and the traditional draughtsmanship. In full consciousness of the risk run, I am prepared to juxtapose a passage from *Emma*, which I believe to be Jane Austen's masterpiece, a passage moreover of consummate art, and a passage from *To the Lighthouse*.

When Emma first becomes acquainted with Harriet, Jane

Austen presents the situation in such a way as to give the reader a clear insight into Emma's character. And with her customary precision and what Virginia Woolf calls her "impeccable sense of human values", she guides the reader's judgment.

"Harriet Smith's intimacy at Hartfield was soon a settled thing. Quick and decided in her ways, Emma lost no time in inviting, encouraging, and telling her to come very often; and as their acquaintance increased, so did their satisfaction in each other. As a walking companion, Emma had very early foreseen how useful she might find her.... She had ventured alone once to Randalls, but it was not pleasant; and a Harriet Smith, therefore, one whom she could summon at any time to a walk, would be a valuable addition to her privileges. But in every respect as she saw more of her, she approved her, and was confirmed in all her kind designs.

"Harriet certainly was not clever, but she had a sweet, docile, grateful disposition, was totally free from conceit, and only desiring to be guided by anyone she looked up to. Her early attachment to herself was very amiable; and her inclination for good company, and power of appreciating what was elegant and clever, showed that there was no want of taste, though strength of understanding must not be expected. Altogether she was quite convinced of Harriet Smith's being exactly the young friend she wanted—exactly the something which her home required."

The first sentence of this passage merely states certain facts; but the second sentence dissects Emma's motives with surgical precision and with subtle artistry.

"...Emma had very early foreseen how *useful...a* Harriet Smith"; by the turn of a phrase, the choice of an indefinite article, Jane Austen guides the reader's judgment and prepares the way for the ironic close of the paragraph: "confirmed in all her kind designs." The opening of the second paragraph can be read as statement of fact by the omniscient narrator; but it is principally an account of Emma's impression of Harriet, "not clever...sweet, docile, grateful...desiring to be guided...". It is Emma, not Jane Austen, who finds Harriet's easily won affection "amiable", and Emma who thinks of herself as "good company...elegant, clever". In the last sentence the effect of the whole paragraph is summed up, and the obtuse egotism with which Emma has chosen a friend is wholly in the reader's grasp for his enjoyment, amusement and judgment, "—exactly the something which her home required".

In the following passage from Virginia Woolf's *To the Lighthouse*, as in the passage from *Emma*, two persons are presented, Mr Tansley and Lily Briscoe. Mr Tansley is a young man researching in a philosophical subject, a disciple of Mr Ramsay, introduced by him into the house party which includes, besides the Ramsay family, several of their intimates. Tansley is comparatively a stranger among them. Lily is a painter and is preoccupied with the painting at which she has been working during the day. The visit to the Lighthouse mentioned in the passage refers back to a proposed expedition on the morrow, which is of considerable importance in the book. The scene is a dinner party and Lily is sitting opposite Mr Tansley.

"Mr Tansley was really, Lily Briscoe thought, in spite of his eyes, but then look at his nose, look at his hands, the most uncharming human being she had ever met. Then why did she mind what he said? Women can't write, women can't paint—what did it matter, coming from him, since clearly it was not true to him but for some reason helpful to him, and that was why he said it? Why did her whole being bow, like corn under a wind, and erect itself again from this abasement only with a great and rather painful effort? She must make it once more. There's the sprig on the tablecloth; there's my painting; I must move the tree to the middle; that matters—nothing else. Could she not hold fast to that, she asked herself, and not lose her temper, and

not argue; and if she wanted a little revenge take it by laughing
at him.

"'Oh, Mr Tansley', she said, 'do take me to the Lighthouse
with you. I should so love it.'

"She was telling lies he could see. She was saying what she
did not mean to annoy him, for some reason. She was laughing
at him. He was in his old flannel trousers. He had no others.
He felt very rough and isolated and lonely. He knew that she
was trying to tease him for some reason; she didn't want to go
to the Lighthouse with him; she despised him: so did Prue
Ramsay; so did they all. But he was not going to be made a fool
of by women, so he turned deliberately in his chair and looked
out of the window and said, all in a jerk, very rudely, it would
be too rough for her tomorrow. She would be sick."

[*To the Lighthouse*]

The most obvious difference between this passage and the one
from *Emma* is that the writer seems to have vanished, we are no
longer aware of a mind directing our judgment. Certainly we
discern an overassertive ego, both in Mr Tansley and in Lily;
but equally certainly we do not judge them. The spirit of comedy
pervades this scene as it does the other; but it is not here satiric
comedy. In the passage from *Emma* we were given certain indica-
tions of what went on in Emma's mind; but it was unmistakably
Jane Austen who selected them and governed our response to
them. In the passage from *To the Lighthouse* we attend exclusively
to the thoughts and the words of Lily and Mr Tansley. But there
is a further and perhaps more significant difference between the
two passages. The extract from Jane Austen is curiously complete
in itself. It almost seems as though the book could be reconstructed from these paragraphs. Emma's attitude to Harriet at
this point in the story epitomizes the error of judgment and the
flaw in her character from which all the complications in the
story and the whole development of the character arise. The

attentive reader has, in this single passage, a key to the whole situation. The passage is centripetal. The passage from Virginia Woolf is centrifugal. Everything in it implies or demands extension out into the rest of the book. More knowledge of the way Lily looks at the world is implied than is given; sufficient understanding of it can only be gathered from the whole book. The remark "Women can't write, women can't paint" recalls, not only a particular utterance but the reader's sense of Lily's self-consciousness which has been gradually formed in preceding episodes and will be extended until the final page. The degree in which she is right in supposing "it was not true to him but for some reason helpful to him", can only be known by reading all that has preceded. The way in which she recovers her balance by forming a new conception of her picture can only be fully appreciated in relation to earlier and later impressions of Lily at work. The visit to the Lighthouse, as has already been suggested, is far richer in significance than the single passage would imply. Similarly with all the impressions of Tansley gained in the last paragraph, none of them can be fully appreciated except in relation to the whole impression of Tansley, which cannot be isolated from the pattern of personalities in which we become aware of him. In this sense it is true to say that the art of Virginia Woolf is not applied to the drawing of single characters.

She was impelled by her own "vision of life" to emphasize the fluidity of human personality rather than its fixity. She perceived the variety of impressions made by one person upon the people round him and his own ever-changing consciousness of the surrounding world. Consequently, instead of defining an identity or epitomizing it in a particular incident, she invites us to discover it by living in the minds of her characters, or in the minds of others with whom they come into contact. The discovery can only be made by a gradually acquired intimacy. Understanding is cumulative. In *Jacob's Room* no very clear picture of Jacob as an individual emerges, because neither he himself nor the minds in which he is reflected are developed sufficiently for us to become intimate with them. On the other hand, in each scene or incident the quality of experience is fully communicated, our interest is concentrated upon modes of feeling that are common to many, rather than on those modes of feeling which define an individual. The power of communicating with profound insight and discriminating exactness experiences which are widespread and produce in the reader a sense of recognition is an essential part of Virginia Woolf's creative gift; though it is not the whole. It is developed to its fullest extent in *The Waves*. In that book she denies herself not only the outlined or summarized character seen from a point of view outside the book, but also the differentiated style in thought or speech, which is an alternative way of demarcating individuality. The six principal characters, from the nursery to old age, express themselves in the same subtle and imaginative idiom. Interest is focused upon their inward experience. Nevertheless, because of the small number of persons presented and the gradual unfolding of their minds, the reader becomes intimate with each and the six are clearly differentiated both from one another and from themselves at the different periods of their lives. The vocabulary, imagery and rhythms with which they are all alike endowed, is an unrealistic convention, which the reader has to accept. But the content of the consciousness expressed by each is always consistent both with the individual and with the time of life. Here, for instance, is the voice of Susan at the end of her school time; looking forward to being at home:

"I shall throw myself on a bank by the river and watch the fish slip in and out among the reeds. The palms of my hands will be printed with pine needles. I shall there unfold and take out whatever it is that I have made here; something hard. For something has grown in me here, through the winters and summers, on staircases, in bedrooms. I do not want, as Jinny wants, to be admired. I do not want people, when I come in, to look up with admiration. I want to give, to be given, and solitude in which to unfold my possessions."

[*The Waves*]

And here is the voice of Susan in middle age:

"Now I measure, I preserve. At night I sit in the arm-chair and stretch my arm for my sewing; and hear my husband snore; and look up when the light from a passing car dazzles the windows and feel the waves of my life tossed, broken, round me who am rooted; and hear cries, and see others' lives eddying like straws round the piers of a bridge while I push my needle in and draw my thread through the calico.

"I think sometimes of Percival who loved me. He rode and fell in India. I think sometimes of Rhoda. Uneasy cries wake me at dead of night. But for the most part I walk content with my sons. I cut the dead petals from hollyhocks. Rather squat, grey before my time, but with clear eyes, pear-shaped eyes, I pace my fields."

[*The Waves*]

But the voice of Rhoda is different. Here is Rhoda at school:

"'That is my face', said Rhoda, 'in the looking glass behind Susan's shoulder—that face is my face. But I will duck behind her to hide it, for I am not here. I have no face. Other people have faces; Susan and Jinny have faces; they are here. Their world is the real world. The things they lift are heavy. They say Yes, they say No; whereas I shift and change and am seen through in a second. If they meet a housemaid she looks at them without laughing. But she laughs at me. They know what to say if spoken to. They laugh really; they get angry really; while I have to look first and do what other people do when they have done it.'"

[*The Waves*]

And this is the voice of Rhoda, the woman:

"Oh, life, how I have dreaded you...oh, human beings how I have hated you! How you have nudged, how you have interrupted, how hideous you have looked in Oxford Street, how squalid sitting opposite each other staring in the Tube!...How you snatched from me the white spaces that lie between hour and hour and rolled them into dirty pellets and tossed them into the waste paper basket with your greasy paws. Yet those were my life.

"But I yielded. Sneers and yawns were covered with my hand. I did not go out into the street and break a bottle in the gutter as a sign of rage. Trembling with ardour, I pretended that I was not surprised. If Susan and Jinny pulled up their stockings like that, I pulled mine up like that also. So terrible was life that I held up shade after shade. Look at life through this, look at life through that; let there be rose leaves, let there be vine leaves— I covered the whole street, Oxford Street, Piccadilly Circus, with the blaze and ripple of my mind, with vine leaves and rose leaves."

[The Waves]

The disadvantage of the convention adopted in *The Waves*, as regards character creation, is not that the six persons are undifferentiated, but rather the reverse. Because they are all endowed with an idiom suited to the expression of a subtle self-awareness, and so cannot be recognized by their accent nor by the form of their thought, the distinguishing quality of their personality has to be strongly emphasized; each is attached to his or her own symbol. Bernard is tied to his curiosity, his phrase-making, his desire to find a "story"; Susan to her need to strike roots, to possess, "to give, to be given"; Rhoda to her dreams and her fear of life; Jinny to her sensuousness and need for admiration; Neville to his love of order and intellectual clarity; Louis to his social insecurity, his "Australian accent and his father a banker in Brisbane", but also to "the great beast stamping", to his sense of identity with the past history of the race:

34

"What has my destiny been, the sharp-pointed pyramid that has pressed on my ribs all these years? That I remember the Nile and the women carrying pitchers on their heads; that I feel myself woven in and out of the long summers and winters that have made the corn flow and have frozen the streams. I am not a single and passing being. My life is not a moment's bright spark like that on the surface of the diamond. I go beneath ground tortuously, as if a warder carried a lamp from cell to cell. My destiny has been that I remember and must weave together, must plait into one cable the many threads, the thin, the thick, the broken, the enduring of our long history, of our tumultuous and varied day...."   [*The Waves*]

It does not matter that, in this book, the characters have depth rather than width. The narrowing *leit-motif* helps to keep each distinct and also to weave the pattern of the whole. The reader is not disturbed by the emphasis on a defining attitude to life, because he is not, for the time being, attending to characterization but to human experience. He is attending to what it feels like to be young, or middle aged, or old; to be in the country or at school or in a London street; to rejoice, or to suffer, to strive or to be serene. The six personalities, with their differences of temperament, are the vehicles by which the experience is brought to him. The excitement of reading *The Waves* is due to an extension of ourselves, a quickening of memory and a deepening of perception, rather than to an addition to that gallery of human portraits to which fiction usually contributes.

But, although this subjective element is always important, it is not elsewhere so predominant as in *The Waves*. Virginia Woolf, in her other books, expresses more fully the diversity within unity of individual human beings, and differentiation of character is not elsewhere confined to a symbolic hall mark. The peculiar quality of *The Waves* required this device; with it she succeeded in communicating the gradual unfolding of human consciousness from youth to age in modern men and women with a similar cultural background and a similar endowment of sensibility and intelligence. She sacrificed some aspects of her vision so that the reader might live more fully within the minds of her six characters from youth to age. In all her novels, after the first two, personality is revealed as much by the record of an inner monologue as by action and conversation; but elsewhere the characters are more completely given. This is achieved by a continual shifting from mind to mind, so that we as often observe the experience given by one to another as the experience each receives. Also certain scenes are selected which throw a character into high relief, the scenes between Mrs Dalloway and Miss Kilman, for instance, or between Lucy Swithin and William Dodge in *Between the Acts*. But in *The Waves* certain characters and events that affect the central six are in partial or complete shadow; Susan's husband, Bernard's wife, Neville's male and Louis's female lovers (other than those from among the six) are completely unknown to the reader. Even Percival, who plays so important a part in all their lives, is given only as a type. In *To the Lighthouse*, on the other hand, our considerable knowledge of Mr Ramsay is an important factor in our understanding of his wife; Mrs Ramsay's effect upon Lily, Mr Bankes, Mr Carmichael, Mr Tansley or her own children forms an integral part of the reader's impression of her personality. Similarly, Mrs Dalloway emerges as a fully rounded character because we know her husband, and Peter Walsh, Miss Kilman and Sally Seton and several others in whose minds we see her reflected. And we are present, either directly or by sharing the memories of divers people, at a number of crucial moments in her life, in which her personality expresses itself. Lucy Swithin in *Between the Acts* is known by her relation with her brother, with her daughter-in-law, with William Dodge and others, because we also know them. So it is with other characters in these books. It is not,

I think, true of them that "they cannot be remembered afterwards on their own account". It is partially true of the characters in *The Waves* because the human value of that book is of a different kind.

The Waves is the fullest expression of the subjective aspect of Virginia Woolf's creative genius; in it the attention is wholly concentrated upon six people, and human experience is revealed from within their minds. In that book minor characters are very nearly non-existent. In *The Years*, which followed next and was published six years later, there are a larger number of minor characters than in any other of her books. Just as, in life, people less intimately known to us are more easily defined, so it is with the minor character in fiction. As with comparative strangers, so with these background characters, the more distant viewpoint obscures the finely shaded, ever-varying quality of human personality—what is seen is the firm contour, the typical appearance and behaviour. The older method of character drawing, whose linear ancestor is the Theophrastian character, is here appropriate. Such characters can be conveyed by description and by a selection of typical speech and action. So, in *The Years*, whereas we live within the minds of the principals, the host of other people who surround them and contribute to the pattern of their lives are described from without. Colonel Abel Pargiter visits his mistress and her *character* and physical environment are firmly and quickly sketched:

"Nobody was there; he was too early. He looked round the room with distaste. There were too many little objects about. He felt out of place, and altogether too large as he stood upright before the draped fireplace in front of a screen upon which was painted a kingfisher in the act of alighting on some bulrushes. Footsteps scurried about hither and thither on the floor above. Was there somebody with her? he asked himself listening. Children screamed in the street outside. It was sordid; it was mean; it was furtive. One of these days, he said to himself. . . but the door opened and his mistress, Mira, came in.

"'Oh Bogy, dear!' she exclaimed. Her hair was very untidy;

37

she was a little fluffy-looking; but she was very much younger than he was and really glad to see him, he thought. The little dog bounced up at her.

"'Lulu, Lulu', she cried, catching the little dog in one hand while she put the other to her hair, 'come and let Uncle Bogy look at you.'"

[*The Years*]

The Years is not wholly successful because, with so large a canvas and so many background and foreground characters, the reader's attention is insufficiently centred. As in *Jacob's Room*, the first experiment in the new form, so here, in the first attempt to combine the advantages of the new presentation of character with those of the old, individual scenes and experiences are vivid, rich and delicately observed; but the book, even after several readings, does not give the reader the sense of a single, organized whole. In her next and last book, *Between the Acts*, the problem of combining, without confusion, subjective revelation of personality with definition of minor characters is solved by the invention of a subtle and complex form. Within that form both methods of characterization are successfully used; Mrs Manresa, for instance, is shown directly by the author, or reflected in the minds of the other characters, or by her words and actions—at moments even, though much more rarely than with the people we know more intimately, we live in her own mind:

"Then they went in to lunch, and Mrs Manresa bubbled up, enjoying her own capacity to surmount, without turning a hair, this minor social crisis—this laying of two more places. For had she not complete faith in flesh and blood? and aren't we all flesh and blood? and how silly to make bones of trifles when we are all flesh and blood under the skin—men and women too! But she preferred men—obviously.

"Or what are your rings for, and your nails, and that really adorable little straw hat?" said Isa addressing Mrs Manresa silently and thereby making silence add its unmistakable contribution to talk. Her hat, her rings, her finger nails red as roses, smooth as shells, were there for all to see. But not her life history. That was only scraps and fragments to all of them, excluding perhaps William Dodge, whom she called 'Bill' publicly—a sign perhaps that he knew more than they did. Some of the things that he knew—that she strolled the garden at midnight in silk pyjamas, had the loud-speaker playing jazz, and a cocktail bar, of course they knew also. But nothing private; no strictly biographical facts."

[*Between the Acts*]

There follows a paragraph, still expressing what goes on in Isa's mind, giving a few conjectural details of Mrs Manresa's biography. After which Mrs Manresa speaks:

"'All I need,' said Mrs Manresa ogling Candish, as if he were a real man, not a stuffed man, 'is a corkscrew.'

"'Look, Bill', she continued, cocking her thumb—she was opening the bottle—'at the pictures. Didn't I tell you you'd have a treat?'

"Vulgar she was in her gestures, in her whole person, over-sexed, over-dressed for a picnic. But what a desirable, at least valuable, quality it was—for everybody felt, directly she spoke, 'She's said it, she's done it, not I', and could take advantage of the breach of decorum, of the fresh air that blew in, to follow like leaping dolphins in the wake of an ice-breaking vessel. Did she not restore to old Bartholomew his spice islands, his youth?

"'I told him', she went on, ogling Bart now, 'that he wouldn't look at our things' (of which they had heaps and mountains) 'after yours. And I promised him you'd show him the — the —', here the champagne fizzed up and she insisted upon filling Bart's glass first. 'What is it all you learned gentlemen rave about? An arch? Norman? Saxon? Who's the last from school? Mrs Giles?'

"She ogled Isabella now, conferring youth upon her; but always when she spoke to women, she veiled her eyes, for they, being conspirators, saw through it.

"So with blow after blow, with champagne and ogling, she staked out her claim to be a wild child of nature."

[*Between the Acts*]

39

With such variety and flexibility of method Mrs Manresa is presented; a minor character in the sense that we do not wholly identify ourselves with her, yet a memorable and important character who plays an essential part in the whole composition.

Like most novelists, Virginia Woolf can only fully communicate the experience of a limited number of human types. Some great novelists have a wider, some a narrower range than hers. By enriching her technique of character drawing in *Between the Acts*, she was able to extend her range; but in the main, because she focused her vision of human beings upon the indefinable, fluid personality, rather than on the definite and settled *character*, she concentrated upon those kinds of people into whose minds she could most fully enter and through whose eyes she could imagine herself looking out upon the world. For her central characters she limits herself to one large social class, the class of those who have incomes or earn salaries. Around that centre she creates the poor whom Eleanor visits in *The Years*, Mrs Potter, old, deaf and bedridden, or Mrs Dempster and other typical Londoners in *Mrs Dalloway*, and they are often created with the same insight and sureness of touch as the central characters, though with less fullness. Mrs Dempster has a long monologue, of which the following is a sample:

"For it's been a hard life, thought Mrs Dempster. What hadn't she given to it? Roses; figure; her feet too. (She drew the knobbed lumps beneath her skirt.)

"Roses, she thought sardonically. All trash m'dear. For really, what with eating, drinking, and mating, the bad days and good, life had been no mere matter of roses, and what was more, let me tell you, Carrie Dempster had no wish to change her lot with any woman's in Kentish Town...." [*Mrs Dalloway*]

And Virginia Woolf creates also those who are in more direct touch with her centre; Mrs Dalloway's maid Lucy; Crosby, the faithful retainer in *The Years*; the two charwomen in *To the Lighthouse*; the butler, the cook and the villagers in *Between the Acts*. She lives centred, as most people do, in one social sphere and looks outward from it, with sympathy and understanding, but with inevitably diminishing vision, to the spheres outside it.

Like many other novelists, Virginia Woolf also creates a limited range of intellectual and moral types. Jane Austen, for instance, has her intelligent, quick-witted young women, of Elizabeth Bennet's sisterhood, and also those who like Anne Elliot and Fanny Price are more notable for their gentle thoughtfulness; and she has her silly girls and silly women; her vulgarians and her social snobs, both of the climbing and of the condescending, variety. It would be possible also to classify her male characters under some half-dozen heads. Yet she never repeats herself; no individual within the class is mistakable for another. Similarly with Virginia Woolf. There are the disinterested scholars, like Mr Ramsay, Mr Hilbery or Edward Pargiter; there are the intellectuals, who cannot fall in love with the other sex, Bonamy in *Jacob's Room*, Neville in *The Waves*, Nicholas in *The Years* and William Dodge in *Between the Acts*; there are the women with a gift for creating harmony, women of exquisite tact and sensibility like Mrs Ramsay, Mrs Dalloway and Mrs Hilbery; and there are those who create works of art, like Lily Briscoe or Miss La Trobe; and those who work for a cause, like Rose Pargiter in *The Years* and Lady Bruton in *Mrs Dalloway*. These and some few other kinds of person recur in different books; but though they can be roughly classified in this way the individuals within each kind are more unlike than they are like one another. Her range is limited in so far as she sees most clearly, because she sympathises most fully, with men and women who are either sensitive or intelligent or both, and the dimmer wits and, above all, blunter sensibilities are further removed from her centre of vision.

CHAPTER III

STORIES AND SEQUENCES

In the novel before Henry James a sequence of events leading up to a climax and then to a dénouement normally provided the structure within which the whole subject was contained. The novel told a story. After *Night and Day* the novels of Virginia Woolf cease to tell stories. The sequence of events no longer leads to a climax and in the final pages no knot is unravelled:

"But what are stories? Toys I twist, bubbles I blow, one ring passes through another. And sometimes I begin to doubt if there are stories" muses Bernard in *The Waves*.

Virginia Woolf abandoned the convention of the story for the same reason that she abandoned the convention of character drawing; neither of them could be made to express life as she saw it. But it is essential to be clear, even at the risk of repetition, precisely what is meant by character and story. She ceased to draw characters in outline, she ceased to sum up men and women or to give her readers the illusion that they could be covered with a formula, or that their identity was constant and definable. Yet it is no less true of her novels than of those of Jane Austen or George Eliot, that the reader's interest is centred in human beings. Similarly, the reader's attention is still held by the experiences of those human beings, their joy and sorrow, hope and despair. Yet if by a story we mean a connected series of events moving towards a conclusion then (after *Night and Day*) she tells no stories. The events she notes are not always the immediate causes or consequences of other events in the book. Their importance depends upon their effect in the consciousness of her creatures and not upon their function in a plot. No complication is formed to be subsequently unravelled. Nothing is concluded. The sequence of scenes is ordered by their emotional relevance to one another rather than by their logical interrelation. As in her conception of human personality, so in her conception of human experience, continuity and fluidity is emphasized rather than boundary or definition. Often her characters express a sense of life's inconclusiveness or shapelessness, but, for the reader, the rhythm of their experience, the sequence of selected moments in which they are seen provides a structure within which the quality of their living is perceived. When Eleanor looks back over her life in the last chapter of *The Years* she seeks vainly for its form and substance:

"My life, she said to herself. That was odd, it was the second time that evening that somebody had talked about her life. And I haven't got one, she thought. Oughtn't a life to be something you could handle and produce?—a life of seventy odd years. But I've only the present moment, she thought. Here she was alive, now, listening to the fox-trot. Then she looked round. There was Morris; Rose; Edward with his head thrown back talking to a man she did not know. I'm the only person here, she thought, who remembers how he sat on the edge of my bed that night, crying—the night Kitty's engagement was announced. Yes, things came back to her. A long strip of life lay behind her. Edward crying, Mrs Levy talking; snow falling; a sunflower with a crack in it; the yellow omnibus trotting along the Bayswater Road. And I thought to myself, I'm the youngest person in this omnibus; now I'm the oldest.... Millions of things came back to her. Atoms danced apart and massed themselves. But how did they compose what people called a life? She clenched her hands and felt the hard little coins she was holding. Perhaps there's 'I' at the middle of it, she thought; a knot; a centre; and again she saw herself sitting at her table drawing on

43

the blotting paper, digging little holes from which spokes radiated. Out and out they went; thing followed thing, scene obliterated scene. And then they say, she thought, 'We've been talking about you!'"

[*The Years*]

Eleanor's life story, as told in *The Years*, is not "something you could handle or produce". It has consisted of a series of impressions, vividly memorable for the reader. And it has consisted of the impact upon her of other personalities whose names in this passage evoke the scenes she recalls. The elements do not compose a story from which a conclusion can be drawn as, for instance, George Eliot draws her conclusion when the life of Dorothea is contemplated at the close of *Middlemarch*.

"Dorothea herself had no dreams of being praised above other women, feeling that there was always something better which she might have done, if she had only been better and known better. Still she never repented that she had given up position to marry Will Ladislaw, and he would have held it the greatest shame as well as sorrow to him if she had repented. They were bound to each other by a love stronger than any impulses which could have marred it. No life would have been possible to Dorothea which was not filled with emotion, and she had now a life filled also with a beneficent activity which she had not the doubtful pains of discovering and marking out for herself. Will became an ardent public man, working well in those times when reforms were begun with a young hopefulness of immediate good which has been much checked in our days, and getting at last returned to Parliament by a constituency who paid his expenses. Dorothea would have liked nothing better, since wrongs existed, than that her husband should be in the thick of a struggle against them, and that she should give him wifely help. Many who knew her, thought it a pity that so substantive and rare a creature should have been absorbed into the life of another, and be only known in a certain circle as a wife and mother. But no one stated exactly what else that was in her

44

power she ought rather to have done—not even Sir James
Chetham who went no further than the negative prescription
that she ought not to have married Will Ladislaw."

[*Middlemarch*, George Eliot]

This paragraph implies that something has been completed.
Instead of looking back upon a sequence of "present moments"
we look back upon a continuous and rounded whole. Dorothea's
first marriage, her widowhood, her relations with Ladislaw, her
aspirations and sympathies have led her to this haven of a happy
and beneficent marriage. The stories interwoven in *Middlemarch*,
related as they are to the central story of Dorothea, combine to
compose a structure within which George Eliot communicates
her sense of character and values. We look back with the author
over her whole invention, with its enthralling complications and
its comic and tragic incidents, and we see whither it was all
tending. But in Virginia Woolf's novels, because there is no
completed story, there is no summing up. Moreover, the writer
no longer stands outside her invention pointing to it. Our consciousness of events, in Virginia Woolf's later novels, like our
consciousness of people, is derived, as it seems, directly, from
sharing the experiences of the group who compose the book.

The events which constitute the plot of a traditional novel,
such as a quarrel between lovers, a reconciliation, a marriage or a
death are, from *Jacob's Room* onward, submerged beneath the
current of life. Mrs Flanders has lost her husband Seabrook
before the book opens, at the close her three sons are fighting—
Jacob is to die fighting and, one night at Scarborough, she
hears the guns:

"'The guns?' said Betty Flanders, half asleep, getting out of
bed and going to the window, which was decorated with a
fringe of dark leaves.

"'Not at this distance', she thought. 'It is the sea.'

"Again, far away, she heard the dull sound, as if nocturnal women were beating great carpets. There was Morty lost, and Seabrook dead; her sons fighting for their country. But were the chickens safe? Was that some one moving downstairs? Rebecca with the toothache? No. The nocturnal women were beating great carpets. Her hens shifted slightly on their perches."

[*Jacob's Room*]

There is a profound truth in Virginia Woolf's vision of the experience of the deepest of all sorrows, the death of those we love. What she shows is the continuation of life, the healing tyranny of habit and of the small, unavoidable demands made by living. She does not minimize the pain, but she shows it as it is, continuous, and yet frequently submerged. In *The Waves* Percival is thrown from his horse in India and killed at the age of twenty-five; Percival who was loved by the six characters in whose minds we live throughout the book. And Bernard explores his own grief:

"'Such is the incomprehensible combination', said Bernard, 'such is the complexity of things, that as I descend the staircase I do not know which is sorrow, which joy. My son is born; Percival is dead. I am upheld by pillars, shored up on either side by stark emotions; but which is sorrow, which is joy? I ask, and do not know, only that I need silence, and to be alone and to go out, and to save one hour to consider what has happened to my world, what death has done to my world.'"

[*The Waves*]

And at first everything seems to be changed for him, then life begins to take hold of him again:

"'Yet already signals begin, beckonings, attempts to lure me back. Curiosity is knocked out only for a short time. One cannot live outside the machine for more than perhaps half an hour. Bodies, I note, already begin to look ordinary; but what is behind them differs—the perspective. Behind that newspaper

46

placard is the hospital; the long room with black men pulling ropes; and then they bury him. Yet since it says a famous actress has been divorced, I ask instantly Which? Yet I cannot take out my penny; I cannot buy a paper; I cannot suffer interruption yet."

[*The Waves*]

That is how the rhythm of life reasserts itself for Bernard because for Bernard, the weaver of stories, curiosity is a mainspring of life. For the other five characters life resumes its sway differently, for all the death of Percival is a bitter experience; but it solves nothing and it concludes nothing for them, the pain is absorbed into their lives. It is absorbed but it has become part of them. The pain endures. When, in the last section of the book, Bernard, now an old man, at the point of death, looks back, the life and death of Percival are seen as a dominant, recurrent theme in the whole symphony of his experience. First he recalls Percival the boy, and how he felt about him then, and so moves on to Percival, the young man, and to his death:

"Percival sat staring straight ahead of him that day in chapel. He also had a way of flicking his hand to the back of his neck. His movements were always remarkable. We all flicked our hands to the back of our heads—unsuccessfully. He had the kind of beauty which defends itself from any caress. As he was not in the least precocious, he read whatever was written up for our edification without any comment, and thought with that magnificent equanimity (Latin words come naturally) that was to preserve him from so many meannesses and humiliations, that Lucy's flaxen pigtails and pink cheeks were the height of female beauty. Thus preserved, his taste later was of extreme fineness. But there should be music, some wild carol. Through the window should come a hunting song from some rapid unapprehended life—a sound that shouts among the hills and dies away. What is startling, what is unexpected, what we cannot account for, what turns symmetry to nonsense—that comes suddenly to my mind, thinking of him. . . . He was thrown, riding in a race, and when

47

I came along Shaftesbury Avenue tonight those insignificant and scarcely formulated faces that bubble up out of the doors of the Tube, and many obscure Indians, and people dying of famine and disease, and women who have been cheated, and whipped dogs and crying children—all these seemed to me bereft. He would have done justice. He would have protected. About the age of forty he would have shocked the authorities. No lullaby has ever occurred to me capable of singing him to rest."   [*The Waves*]

This is Bernard's sense of what Percival was, and what the world lost in him. Later we are given more poignantly the personal loss. He remembers being with Neville and as he left him, making way for one of Neville's lovers:

"Heavens! how they caught me as I left the room, the fangs of that old pain! the desire for someone not there. For whom? I did not know at first; then remembered Percival. I had not thought of him for months. Now to laugh with him, to laugh with him at Neville—that was what I wanted, to walk off arm in arm together laughing. But he was not there. The place was empty.

"It is strange how the dead leap out on us at street corners, or in dreams."   [*The Waves*]

Perhaps the most moving account of the experience of the death of a person loved is the death of the shell-shocked Septimus Warren Smith in *Mrs Dalloway*. No extract can convey the whole of its effect upon the reader because here, as in *The Waves*, the book is a closely woven pattern in which every part is dependent, for its total effect, upon the rest. But it may be possible to illustrate both the way in which such an experience is communicated as a part of the texture of living, rather than as the climax or conclusion of a story, and also the way in which the sequence of experiences in which it figures governs the reader's response to the single event. Earlier scenes have shown the agonized distress of Septimus's young Italian wife Rezia, alone in London with her husband who is on the brink of a complete mental breakdown; and the reader has felt the full horror of the doctor's clumsy and complacent attempts to help. Then there comes an oasis of happiness for Rezia. For a brief space Septimus recovers his sanity. Rezia sits trimming a hat, and Septimus watches her and jokes with her as he used to do:

"They were perfectly happy now, she said suddenly, putting the hat down. For she could say anything to him now. She could say whatever came into her head. That was almost the first thing she had felt about him, that night in the café when he had come in with his English friends. He had come in, rather shyly, looking round him, and his hat had fallen when he hung it up. That she could remember. She knew he was English, though not one of the large Englishmen her sister admired, for he was always thin; but he had a beautiful fresh colour; and with his big nose, his bright eyes, his way of sitting a little hunched, made her think, she had often told him, of a young hawk, that first evening she saw him, when they were playing dominoes, and he had come in—of a young hawk; but with her he was always very gentle. She had never seen him wild or drunk, only suffering sometimes through this terrible war, but even so, when she came in, he would put it all away. Anything, anything in the whole world, any little bother with her work, anything that struck her to say she would tell him, and he understood at once. Her own family even were not the same. Being older than she was and being so clever—how serious he was, wanting her to read Shakespeare before she could even read a child's story in English!—being so much more experienced he could help her. And she, too, could help him."   [Mrs Dalloway]

But the great nerve specialist, Sir William Bradshaw, has decreed that Septimus must be separated from her. He must go into an institution. And presently the step of Dr Holmes is heard on the stair and Rezia, with her sure instinct, goes out to try and stop him from breaking through her husband's tenuous hold on sanity. Septimus overhears their conversation on the stairs, he knows that the doctors will inevitably win; and he throws himself from the window:

"Rezia ran to the window, she saw; she understood. Dr Holmes and Mrs Filmer collided with each other. Mrs Filmer flapped her apron and made her hide her eyes in the bedroom. There was a great deal of running up and down stairs. Dr Holmes came in—white as a sheet, shaking all over, with a glass in his hand. She must be brave and drink something, he said (What was it? Something sweet), for her husband was horribly mangled, would not recover consciousness, she must not see him, must be spared as much as possible, would have the inquest to go through, poor young woman. Who could have foretold it? A sudden impulse, no one was in the least to blame (he told Mrs Filmer). And why the devil he did it, Dr Holmes could not conceive.

"It seemed to her as she drank the sweet stuff that she was opening long windows, stepping out into some garden. But where? The clock was striking—one, two, three: how sensible the sound was compared with all this thumping and whispering; like Septimus himself. She was falling asleep. But the clock went on striking, four, five, six and Mrs Filmer waving her apron (they wouldn't bring the body in here would they?) seemed part of that garden; or a flag. She had once seen a flag slowly rippling out from a mast when she stayed with her aunt at Venice. Men killed in battle were thus saluted, and Septimus had been through the War. Of her memories most were happy....

    *   *   *   *   *

"'He is dead', she said, smiling at the poor old woman who guarded her with her honest light-blue eyes fixed on the door. (They wouldn't bring him in here, would they?) But Mrs Filmer pooh-poohed. Oh no, oh no! They were carrying him away now. Ought she not to be told? Married people ought to be together, Mrs Filmer thought. But they must do as the doctor said.

"'Let her sleep', said Dr Holmes, feeling her pulse. She saw the large outline of his body dark against the window. So that was Dr Holmes." [*Mrs Dalloway*]

The tragic story of Septimus does not provide the structural outline of the book; it is inwoven with the whole pattern of selected human experiences whose relation to one another is emotional rather than logical. The pattern is composed of sequences rather than consequences. Immediately before the scene between Rezia and Septimus, of which these extracts are a fragment, the reader is in the street with Elizabeth Dalloway and her youthful hopes and aspirations; her projection of her own happiness into the world without has an emotional relevance to the last phase of the life of Septimus, though she knows nothing of his existence:

"...She penetrated a little farther in the direction of St Paul's. She liked the geniality, sisterhood, motherhood, brotherhood of this uproar. It seemed to her good. The noise was tremendous; and suddenly there were trumpets (the unemployed) blaring, rattling about in the uproar; military music; as if people were marching; yet had they been dying—had some woman breathed her last, and whoever was watching, opening the window of the room where she had just brought off that act of supreme dignity, looked down on Fleet Street, that uproar, that military music would have come triumphing up to him, consolatory, indifferent.

"It was not conscious. There was no recognition in it of one's fortune, or fate, and for that very reason even to those dazed with watching for the last shivers of consciousness on the faces of the dying, consoling.

"Forgetfulness in people might wound, their ingratitude corrode, but this voice pouring endlessly, year in year out, would take whatever it might be; this vow; this van; this life; this procession, would wrap them all about and carry them on, as in the rough stream of a glacier the ice holds a splinter of bone, a blue petal, some oak trees, and rolls them on." [Mrs Dalloway]

Elizabeth Dalloway's sense of the consolatory grandeur of the endless hubbub of the city and her perception of individual human sorrows preserved and submerged in the stream of time, is related by a poetic logic to the death of Septimus:

"But it was later than she thought. Her mother would not like her to be wandering off alone like this. She turned back down the Strand.

"A puff of wind (in spite of the heat there was quite a wind) blew a thin black veil over the sun and over the Strand. The faces faded; the omnibuses suddenly lost their glow. For although the clouds were of mountainous white so that one could fancy hacking hard chips off with a hatchet, with broad golden slopes, lawns of celestial pleasure gardens, on their flanks, and had all the appearance of settled habitations assembled for the conference of gods above the world, there was a perpetual movement among them. Signs were interchanged, when, as if to fulfil some scheme arranged already, now a summit dwindled, now a whole block of pyramidal size which had kept its station unalterably advanced into the midst or gravely led the procession to fresh anchorage. Fixed though they seemed at their posts, at rest in perfect unanimity, nothing could be fresher, freer, more sensitive superficially than the snow-white or gold-kindled surface; to change, to go, to dismantle the solemn assemblage was immediately possible; and in spite of the grave fixity, the accumulated robustness and solidity, now they struck light to the earth, now darkness.

"Calmly and competently, Elizabeth Dalloway mounted the Westminster omnibus." [Mrs Dalloway]

The cloudscape not only symbolizes the alternating light and darkness of human experience, it also provides the immediate link between Elizabeth and Septimus who, looking at the objects in his room, perceives the effects of the same changing light:

"Going and coming, beckoning, signalling, so the light and shadow, which now made the wall grey, now the bananas bright yellow, now made the Strand grey, now made the omnibuses bright yellow, seemed to Septimus Warren Smith lying on the sofa in the sitting-room; watching the watery gold glow and fade with the astonishing sensibility of some live creature on the roses, on the wall-paper. Outside the trees dragged their leaves like nets through the depths of the air, the sound of water was in the room, and through the waves came the voices of birds singing. Every power poured its treasures on his head, and his hand lay there on the back of the sofa, as he had seen his hand lie when he was bathing, floating, on the top of the waves, while far away on shore he heard dogs barking and barking far away. Fear no more, says the heart in the body; fear no more."

"He was not afraid. At every moment Nature signified by some laughing hint like that gold spot which went round the wall—there, there, there—her determination to show, by brandishing her plumes, shaking her tresses, flinging her mantle this way and that, beautifully, always beautifully, and standing close up to breathe through her hollowed hands Shakespeare's words, her meaning.

"Rezia, sitting at the table twisting a hat in her hands, watched him; saw him smiling. He was happy then...."

[Mrs Dalloway]

The same beauty of the day that permeated and governed the musings of Elizabeth gave to Septimus his moment of restored happiness and sanity before death, and that beauty too is the background against which Peter Walsh, into whose mind we pass immediately after the death scene, perceives the ambulance:

"One of the triumphs of civilization, Peter Walsh thought. It is one of the triumphs of civilization as the light high bell of the ambulance sounded. Swiftly, cleanly, the ambulance sped to

53

the hospital, having picked up instantly, humanely, some poor devil; someone hit on the head, struck down by disease, knocked over perhaps a minute or so ago at one of these crossings, as might happen to oneself. That was civilization."   [*Mrs Dalloway*]

There is irony in these juxtapositions; in Elizabeth's transformation of that procession of the unemployed into the "drums and trumpets" of high romance and in Peter's perception of the removal of Septimus's remains as a "triumph of civilization"—a civilization of which the reader knows that Septimus was a tragic victim. But there is also an effect more potent than irony, an effect of the same order as that produced by the transitions in Keats' *Ode to a Nightingale*. Often the form and substance of Virginia Woolf's novels resemble the form and substance of lyrical poetry more closely than they do those of traditional prose fiction. The experiences of death and of love which so often provide the climax of a great story, are, in her books, inwoven with the texture of human life and so placed that suffering, or joy, beauty or ugliness perplex and quicken the mind and

> "tease us out of thought
> As doth eternity."

In her first novel, *The Voyage Out*, love and death close the story. In *Night and Day*, that rich and fascinating book, in which the new wine of her individual vision of life is imperfectly contained within the old bottle of the traditional form, the love theme is paramount. There are five lovers, Katharine Hilbery, Ralph Denham, William Rodney, Cassandra Otway and Mary Datchet; in the traditional way, the story complicates and explicates their relations with one another. As with all good stories, the reader is beguiled by the question "what happened?" Will Katharine marry Rodney, or Ralph? Will Rodney marry Katharine or Cassandra? Will Ralph marry Mary or Katharine? All these possibilities lie open almost to the last. But there are other and more important questions raised. What is love? Is it an illusion, or the only reality? Is the lover attracted, or repelled and frightened by the object of his love? Is sympathy and under-standing the root of love or is it remoteness and mystery? Is it intuition that governs choice, or is it reason? After Katharine has become engaged to Rodney she discovers with certainty what all along she suspected, that there is something missing in her feeling about him; but she is not sure whether it is something people dream about or something which exists in normal experience.

"Her aunt's stock of commonplaces, Katharine sometimes suspected, had been laid in on purpose to fill silences with, and had little to do with her private thoughts. But at this moment they seemed terribly in keeping with her own conclusions, so that she took up her knitting again and listened, chiefly with a view to confirming herself in the belief that to be engaged to marry someone with whom you are not in love is an inevitable step in a world where the existence of passion is only a traveller's story brought from the heart of deep forests and told so rarely that wise people doubt whether the story can be true."

[*Night and Day*]

There comes a moment when Katharine sees for herself that the thing exists. Mary tells her of her own love for Ralph Den-ham, and the way she speaks demolishes Katharine's pretence that love is a traveller's tale:

"She sat up straight and looked at me, and then she said, 'I'm in love', Katharine mused, trying to set the whole scene in motion. It was a scene to dwell on with so much wonder that not a grain of pity occurred to her; it was a flame blazing suddenly in the dark; by its light Katharine perceived far too vividly for her comfort the mediocrity, indeed the entirely fictitious character of her own feelings so far as they pretended to correspond with Mary's feelings."

[*Night and Day*]

Already in *Night and Day* the question "What is?" occupies the reader alongside the question "What happens?" There is a structure of several lives woven together into a story: and there are also five different temperaments observing their own experience and trying to discover what it is. Katharine

"thought of three different scenes; she thought of Mary sitting upright and saying, 'I'm in love—I'm in love'; she thought of Rodney losing his self-consciousness among the dead leaves, and speaking with the abandonment of a child; she thought of Denham leaning upon the stone parapet and talking to the distant sky, so that she thought him mad. Her mind, passing from Mary to Denham, from William to Cassandra, and from Denham to herself—if, as she rather doubted, Denham's state of mind was connected with herself—seemed to be tracing out the lines of some symmetrical pattern, some arrangement of life, which invested, if not herself, at least the others, not only with interest, but with a kind of tragic beauty. She had a fantastic picture of them upholding splendid palaces upon their backs. They were the lantern-bearers, whose lights, scattered among the crowd, wove a pattern, dissolving, joining, meeting again in combination. Half forming such conceptions as these in her rapid walk along the dreary streets of South Kensington, she determined that, whatever else might be obscure, she must further the objects of Mary, Denham, William and Cassandra."

[*Night and Day*]

It is not till later that she discovers that she too is a "lantern-bearer".

In the later books we attend almost exclusively to "What is?" and the question "What happened?" is often answered before the book begins. It is not that curiosity that leads us forward, but the other. In what ways do human beings experience all the varieties of love? The choice or the rejection of a mate, is no longer in the foreground. When we cease to be mainly curious about who married whom and to believe, as we read, that the answer to that question is conclusive, we can attend more fully to the other question, what is the nature of the experience of love and what is its rhythm in the whole composition of a life. So we watch Jacob experiencing divers kinds of love; virginal romantic love for Clara, sensual love for Florinda, pitying love for Fanny Elmer, and idealizing love for Sandra Wentworth Williams:

"Very beautiful she looked. With her hands folded she mused, seemed to listen to her husband, seemed to watch the peasants coming down with brushwood on their backs, seemed to notice how the hill changed from blue to black, seemed to discriminate between truth and falsehood, Jacob thought, and crossed his legs suddenly, observing the shabbiness of his trousers."

[*Jacob's Room*]

It is not now the sequel that occupies the mind of the reader, it is the effect of people on Jacob; and the effect that Jacob himself produces upon other people. Mrs Dalloway, in the book that is named after her, is a married woman of fifty with a grown-up daughter. Her love-story, in the old sense, is already completed. But her experience of love is a part of the woof and warp of the book. There is her love for Peter Walsh, both as it was, and as it is:

"Always when she thought of him she thought of their quarrels for some reason—because she wanted his good opinion so much, perhaps. She owed him words: 'sentimental', 'civilized'; they started up every day of her life as if he guarded her. A book was sentimental; an attitude to life sentimental. 'Sentimental', perhaps she was to be thinking of the past. What would he think, she wondered, when he came back?"

[*Mrs Dalloway*]

And then, after an interval filled with other experiences, he comes:

"Now the door opened, and in came—for a single second she could not remember what he was called! so surprised she was to see him, so glad, so shy, so utterly taken aback to have Peter Walsh come to her unexpectedly in the morning!"

[*Mrs Dalloway*]

And she recognizes in him the old familiar gestures, intonations, habits of speech and of thought, and memories flood back upon her; and gradually, by means of those memories, the past is reconstructed for the reader. By the same method we are given Peter's consciousness, past and present, of Clarissa. We are made aware of what he suffered when she refused to marry him and how that experience seemed final, like the end of a story, but how, in fact, it ended nothing. Peter sits in Regent's Park and recalls it all:

"It was awful, he cried, awful, awful!
Still, the sun was hot. Still, one got over things. Still, life had a way of adding day to day. Still, he thought, yawning and beginning to take notice—Regent's Park had changed very little since he was a boy,..." [*Mrs Dalloway*]

The loves that bind human beings one to another are not less significant in Virginia Woolf's novels than in the story books. The love between these two endures and is a part of them. Both experience other loves as well, which are different and exist side by side with this one. There is Clarissa's love for her husband:

"In came Richard, holding out flowers....He was holding out flowers—roses, red and white roses. (But he could not bring himself to say he loved her; not in so many words.)
"But how lovely, she said, taking his flowers. She understood; she understood without his speaking...." [*Mrs Dalloway*]

They talk a little about his work and then he leaves her and she muses:

"There is a dignity in people; a solitude; even between husband and wife a gulf; and that one must respect, thought Clarissa, watching him open the door; for one would not part with it oneself, or take it, against his will, from one's husband, without losing one's independence, one's self-respect—something, after all, priceless.

"He returned with a pillow and a quilt.

"'An hour's complete rest after luncheon', he said. And he went.

"How like him! He would go on saying, 'An hour's complete rest after luncheon' to the end of time, because a doctor had ordered it once. It was like him to take what doctors said literally; part of his adorable, divine simplicity, which no one had to the same extent; which made him go and do the thing while she and Peter frittered their time away bickering. He was already half-way to the House of Commons...."

[*Mrs Dalloway*]

In a similar way we discover the quality of Clarissa's love for Sally Seton, both as it was and as it is, or for her daughter, or of her dislike for her daughter's governess Miss Kilman.

Such inlets as these into the consciousness of human beings and into their experience of one another are what the reader is given in place of dramatic events. In so far as the function of a story in the novel was to arrest and sustain interest, such scenes and moments have taken its place. But in so far as the function of the story was to provide a structure within which the subject could be presented as a single whole, its place is taken by the sequence of such moments, juxtaposed so that each enhances and illuminates the other. In Virginia Woolf's best work, though not, I think, in *Jacob's Room* or in *The Years*, these sequences are woven into a single design. In the two books which fail, to my mind, to achieve an adequate structure, the principle of unity depends upon all the experiences standing in some relation with a single central figure, Jacob or Eleanor. In the other books the form is more disciplined and complex. By divers means a group of human beings is assembled in the foreground, within a narrow framework of time and place, and the reader is continually conscious of wider horizons in the background. The design in *The Waves* is of a rather different kind, but here also the subject is treated within a narrow and exacting formal design. The effect is more complex, more profound and more memorable than is the final effect of *Jacob's Room* or of *The Years*.

The disappearance of "the story" and, therefore, of the reader's curiosity about "what happened next", allows for a fuller communication of the rhythmic ebb and flow of love. The relation between Mr and Mrs Ramsay in *To the Lighthouse*, for instance, is gradually unfolded throughout the book. There is the moment before the dinner party, when Mrs Ramsay's vitality is at ebb-tide and she looks back over her life with a sense of its futility:

"But what have I done with my life? thought Mrs Ramsay, taking her place at the head of the table, and looking at all the plates making white circles on it....At the far end, was her husband, sitting down, all in a heap, frowning. What at? She did not know. She did not mind. She could not understand how she had ever felt any emotion or any affection for him. She had a sense of being past everything, through everything, out of everything, as she helped the soup, as if there was an eddy—there—and one could be in it, or one could be out of it, and she was out of it. It's all come to an end, she thought, while they came in one after another, Charles Tansley—'Sit there, please', she said—Augustus Carmichael—and sat down. And meanwhile she waited, passively, for someone to answer her, for something to happen. But this is not a thing, she thought, ladling out soup, that one says."

[*To the Lighthouse*]

Presently her mood changes, pity revitalizes her, pity, less necessary to him than to her, for Mr Bankes who sits beside her:

"—poor man! who had no wife and no children, and dined alone in lodgings except for to-night; and in pity for him, life

60

being now strong enough to bear her on again, she began all this business, as a sailor not without weariness sees the wind fill his sail and yet hardly wants to be off again and thinks how, had the ship sunk, he would have whirled round and round and found rest on the floor of the sea."
[To the Lighthouse]

And Lily watches the ebb and flow of her life in her and perceives the sequence of her moods:

"Lily Briscoe watched her drifting into that strange no-man's land where to follow people is impossible and yet their going inflicts such a chill on those who watch them that they always try at least to follow them with their eyes as one follows a fading ship until the sails have sunk beneath the horizon.

"How old she looks, how worn she looks, Lily thought, and how remote. Then when she turned to William Bankes, smiling, it was as if the ship had turned and the sun had struck its sails again, and Lily thought with some amusement because she was relieved, Why does she pity him? For that was the impression she gave, when she told him that his letters were in the hall. Poor William Bankes, she seemed to be saying, as if her own weariness had been partly pitying people, and the life in her, her resolve to live again, had been stirred by pity."
[To the Lighthouse]

Before the meal is over Mrs Ramsay's deadness of feeling about her husband has vanished. When the men talk politics she wishes he would speak:

"One word, she said to herself. For if he said a thing, it would make all the difference. He went to the heart of things. He cared about fishermen and their wages. He could not sleep for thinking of them. It was altogether different when he spoke; one did not feel then, pray heaven you don't see how little I care, because one did care. Then, realising that it was because she admired him so much that she was waiting for him to speak, she felt as if somebody had been praising her husband to her and their marriage, and she glowed all over without realising that it was she herself who had praised him."
[To the Lighthouse]

Or there is that earlier scene in which a fuller light is shed on the personality of Mr Ramsay and on the clash, contrast and combination between his masculine sense of fact and her feminine sense of human needs. Her six-year-old son is sitting beside her, cutting out pictures, his whole mind possessed by his desire to visit the Lighthouse on the morrow. Once already his father has, wantonly as the boy feels, destroyed his hope of achieving that goal:

"There wasn't the slightest possible chance that they could go to the Lighthouse to-morrow, Mr Ramsay snapped out irascibly.

"How did he know? she asked. The wind often changed.

"The extraordinary irrationality of her remark, the folly of women's minds enraged him.... She flew in the face of facts, made his children hope what was utterly out of the question, in effect, told lies. He stamped his foot on the stone step 'Damn you,' he said. But what had she said? Simply that it might be fine to-morrow. So it might.

"Not with the barometer falling and the wind due west.

"To pursue truth with such astonishing lack of consideration for other people's feelings, to rend the thin veils of civilization so wantonly, so brutally, was to her so horrible an outrage of human decency that, without replying, dazed and blinded, she bent her head as if to let the pelt of jagged hail, the drench of dirty water, bespatter her unrebuked. There was nothing to be said.

"He stood by her in silence. Very humbly at length, he said that he would step over and ask the Coastguards if she liked.

"There was nobody she reverenced as she reverenced him.

"She was quite ready to take his word for it, she said. Only then they need not cut sandwiches—that was all. They came to her, naturally, since she was a woman, all day long with this and that; one wanting this, another that; the children were growing up; she often felt she was nothing but a sponge sopped full of human emotions. Then he said, Damn you. He said,

It must rain. He said, It won't rain; and instantly a Heaven of security opened before her. There was nobody she reverenced more. She was not good enough to tie his shoe strings, she felt."

[*To the Lighthouse*]

The experience of love, like the experience of death, is shown in Virginia Woolf's books as part of the pattern of human life. Neither is seen as a climax or a conclusion. Instead she portrays alternations between vivid consciousness and numb insensibility, the rhythm of human response to these major sources of joy and of grief.

CHAPTER IV

MORALS AND VALUES

"When philosophy is not consumed in a novel, when we can underline this phrase with a pencil, and cut out that exhortation with a pair of scissors and paste the whole into a system, it is safe to say that there is something wrong with the philosophy or with the novel or with both."

[*The Common Reader: Second Series*]

So writes Virginia Woolf, upon the novels of George Meredith. In her own novels the "philosophy" is "consumed" to an exceptional degree. There are two obvious reasons why it must be so. First, because her whole endeavour is towards understanding rather than judgment, and it is from the judgments, pronounced or implied by authors, that we usually extract their own views upon ethical or philosophical questions; and secondly because, in accordance with her own artistic purposes, she disappears from her books with growing completeness. We attend to the thought and the speech of her persons, but never to her own. Yet this clearly does not mean that her novels are empty of moral and metaphysical ideas.

It is not then for moral precepts nor for a system of metaphysics that her reader will look—if he does so, he will look in vain. But no one can write about human beings without revealing their own sense of values. Much can be discovered from Virginia Woolf's novels about the way she saw things; about what things seemed to her important; about what she valued and what she disliked. One notices that certain themes recur and must therefore have held an important place in her thoughts, and her handling of those themes reveals certain predilections and some-

64

times a peculiar conflict or tension of the mind, as of one poised between two opposed beliefs. Such a tension exists, for instance, in her feeling about life itself. Over and over again the people she creates experience the sense that life is chaotic, fragmentary, disillusioning. And as often they experience the intense joy of living. This tension in her feeling about life is already apparent in *The Voyage Out*. The novel moves between the poles of life and death, Rachel questions and seeks for life's meaning, for an order and beauty in life comparable to what she finds in music. When she plays the listeners sit

"very still, as if they saw a building with spaces and columns succeeding each other rising in the empty space. They began to see themselves and their lives, and the whole of human life advancing very nobly under the direction of the music. They felt themselves ennobled, and when Rachel stopped playing they desired nothing but sleep."

[*The Voyage Out*]

But for Mrs Dalloway, in *The Voyage Out*, mere human living in its disorder and its ugliness is more valuable than the beauty of poetry and the peace of death:

"'At your age', she says to Rachel, 'I only liked Shelley. I can remember sobbing over him in the garden.

> He has outsoared the shadow of our night,
> Envy and calumny and hate and pain—

you remember?

> Can touch him not and torture not again
> From the contagion of the world's slow stain.

How divine!—and yet what nonsense!' She looked lightly round the room. 'I always think it's *living*, not dying, that counts. I really respect some snuffy old stockbroker who's gone on adding up column after column all his days, and trotting back to his villa at Brixton with some old pug dog he worships, and a dreary little wife sitting at the end of the table, and going off to Margate for a fortnight—I assure you I know heaps like that—well, they seem to me *really* nobler than poets whom every one worships, just because they're geniuses and die young. But I don't expect *you* to agree with me!'

"She pressed Rachel's shoulder: 'Um-m-m'—she went on quoting— 'Unrest which men miscall delight—

When you're my age you'll see that the world is *crammed* full of delightful things. I think young people make such a mistake about that—not letting themselves be happy. I sometimes think that happiness is the only thing that counts....'"

[*The Voyage Out*]

Yet when Rachel's search is ended and Terence Hewet, her betrothed lover, sits by her bedside:

"An immense feeling of peace came over Terence, so that he had no wish to move or to speak. The terrible torture and unreality of the last days were over, and he had come out now into perfect certainty and peace. His mind began to work naturally again and with great ease. The longer he sat there the more profoundly he was conscious of the peace invading every corner of his soul."

[*The Voyage Out*]

No solution is offered, no conclusion reached about the value or the horror of life, about the peace or the terror of death; it is merely that both experiences are vividly represented in her books. The significance of life; the significance of death is again the central theme in *Jacob's Room*:

"The magnificent world—the live, sane, vigorous world.... These words refer to the stretch of wood pavement between Hammersmith and Holborn in January between two and three in the morning. That was the ground beneath Jacob's feet. It was healthy and magnificent because one room, above a mews, somewhere near the river, contained fifty excited, talkative, friendly people. And then to stride over the pavement (there was scarcely a cab or a policeman in sight) is of itself exhilarating.... In short all the drums and trumpets were sounding."

[*Jacob's Room*]

It is life as men and women experience it that Virginia Woolf presents in her books; that, she believes, is all we can know, and within it lie both extremes, the sense of life's magnificence, and the sense of life's ugliness and chaos:

"Indeed, drums and trumpets is no phrase. Indeed, Piccadilly and Holborn, and the empty sitting-room with fifty people in it are liable at any moment to blow music into the air. Women perhaps are more excitable than men. It is seldom that any one says anything about it, and to see the hordes crossing Waterloo Bridge to catch the non-stop to Surbiton one might think that reason impelled them. No, no. It is the drums and trumpets. Only, should you turn aside into one of those little bays on the Waterloo Bridge to think the matter over, it will probably seem to you all a muddle—all a mystery."

[*Jacob's Room*]

And for Mrs Ramsay, in *To the Lighthouse*, the muddle and the mystery predominate, although she is one of those women, of whom there are several in these novels, who can create shape and order and harmony out of human relationships. Mrs Ramsay

"took a look at life, for she had a clear sense of it there, something real, something private, which she shared neither with her children nor with her husband. A sort of transaction went on between them, in which she was on one side, and life was on another, and she was always trying to get the better of it, as it was of her; and sometimes they parleyed (when she sat alone); there were, she remembered, great reconciliation scenes; but for the most part, oddly enough, she must admit that she felt this thing that she called life terrible, hostile, and quick to pounce on you if you gave it a chance. There were the eternal problems: suffering; death; the poor."

[*To the Lighthouse*]

In the central section of the same book, where we watch the passage of the years after Mrs Ramsay's death this tension between the love and the fear of life is more fully expressed; it is winter, and

"In those mirrors, the minds of men, in those pools of uneasy water, in which clouds for ever turn and shadows form, dreams persisted, and it was impossible to resist the strange intimation which every gull, flower, tree, man and woman, and the white earth itself seemed to declare (but if questioned at once to withdraw) that good triumphs, happiness prevails, order rules; or to resist the extraordinary stimulus to range hither and thither in search of some absolute good, some crystal of intensity, remote from the known pleasures and familiar virtues, something alien to the processes of domestic life, single, hard, bright, like a diamond in the sand, which would render the possessor secure. Moreover, softened and acquiescent, the spring with her bees humming and gnats dancing threw her cloak about her, veiled her eyes, averted her head, and among passing shadows and flights of small rain seemed to have taken upon her a knowledge of the sorrows of mankind.

"[Prue Ramsay died that summer in some illness connected with childbirth, which was indeed a tragedy, people said. They said nobody deserved happiness more.]" [*To the Lighthouse*]

The personality of Mrs Dalloway, sketched a little satirically in *The Voyage Out*, is developed with full sympathy in the book that goes by her name. She (like Mrs Ramsay, though in this one thing only) is one who loves to create order by uniting human beings. Peter Walsh is critical of her love of social functions and she questions herself, recognizing in this love the centre of her life:

"in her own mind now, what did it mean to her, this thing she called life? Oh, it was very queer. Here was So-and-So in South Kensington; someone up in Bayswater; and somebody else, say, in Mayfair. And she felt quite continuously a sense of their existence; and she felt what a waste; and she felt what a pity; and she felt if only they could be brought together; so she did it. And it was an offering, to combine, to create; but to whom?

"An offering for the sake of offering, perhaps. Anyhow, it was her gift. Nothing else had she of the slightest importance; could not think, write, even play the piano. She muddled Armenians and Turks; loved success; hated discomfort; must be liked; talked oceans of nonsense: and to this day, ask her what the Equator was, and she did not know.

"All the same, that one day should follow another; Wednesday, Thursday, Friday, Saturday; that one should wake up in the morning; see the sky; walk in the park; meet Hugh Whitbread; then suddenly in came Peter; then these roses; it was enough. After that how unbelievable death was !— that it must end; and no one in the whole world would know how she had loved it all; how every instant...." [Mrs Dalloway]

And the exquisite joy of life is not merely talked about but re-created, "proved upon our pulses" in the book. But side by side with it stalks the horror and the chaos; Septimus is overwhelmed by it and courts death. Of his death the wife of Sir William Bradshaw, nerve specialist, speaks at Clarissa's party:

"Lady Bradshaw (poor goose—one didn't dislike her) murmured how, 'just as we were starting, my husband was called up on the telephone, a very sad case. A young man (that is what Sir William is telling Mr Dalloway) had killed himself. He had been in the army.' Oh thought Clarissa, in the middle of my party, here's death, she thought." [Mrs Dalloway]

The conflict between an intense love of life and an equally intense perception of its terror is closely linked, for Virginia Woolf, as for Keats, on the one hand with "an exquisite sense of the luxurious" and on the other with a perception of "the miseries of the world" "here where men sit and hear each other

69

groan". It is pity for human suffering that causes Mrs Ramsay's antagonism to life:

"With her mind she had always seized the fact that there is no reason, order, justice: but suffering, death, the poor. There was no treachery too base for the world to commit; she knew that."

[*To the Lighthouse*]

And Virginia Woolf knew that. So she creates Septimus Warren Smith for whom "The world has raised its whip, where will it descend?" In retrospect she shows us Septimus the romantic, idealistic young man, who loved the poets, who came to London, was a clerk, but attended evening classes and when war broke out volunteered to fight for an England which "consisted almost entirely of Shakespeare's plays" and of the woman who "lectured in the Waterloo Road upon Shakespeare". He was a good soldier, he was promoted, he saw his friend killed, but he survived, only:

"Now that it was all over, truce signed, and the dead buried, he had, especially in the evening, these sudden thunder claps of fear. He could not feel...

"It might be possible, Septimus thought, looking at England from the train window, as they left Newhaven; it might be possible that the world itself is without meaning."

[*Mrs Dalloway*]

The two forms of human misery that most haunt the books are poverty and war. War that swallows up Jacob, that destroys Septimus, that tortures the mind of Maggie's husband Renny in *The Years*: after an air raid in 1917:

"They listened. The guns were still firing, but far away in the distance. There was a sound like the breaking of waves on a shore far away.

"'They're only killing other people', said Renny savagely. He kicked the wooden box.

"'But you must let us think of something else', Eleanor protested. The mask had come down over his face." [*The Years*]

War again, the overhanging shadow of impending war, in
Between the Acts, blotting out present joy for Giles who can
hardly mask his

"rage with old fogies who sat and looked at views over coffee
and cream when the whole of Europe—over there—was bristling
like....He had no command of metaphor. Only the ineffective
word 'hedgehog' illustrated his vision of Europe, bristling with
guns, poised with planes. At any moment guns would rake that
land into furrows; planes splinter Bolney Minster into smithereens
and blast the Folly. He, too, loved the view. And blamed Aunt
Lucy, looking at views, instead of—doing what?"

[*Between the Acts*]

Similar to the tension in the novels between the love and the
hatred of life, is the tension between doing and contemplating.
It is the nature of the artist to contemplate and re-create the
human scene, not to endeavour to change it. He is endowed with
what Keats calls "negative capability"; he is "capable of being
in uncertainties, mysteries, doubts, without any irritable reaching
after fact and reason...with a great poet the sense of Beauty
overcomes every other consideration". Virginia Woolf is among
those poets whom Keats admires, who have "no palpable design
upon us". Yet the poet is not less, but more conscious of the
world about him than the average man; therefore to him

"the miseries of the world
Are misery, and will not let him rest."

Like Keats, Virginia Woolf feels sometimes that

"there is no worthy pursuit but the idea of doing some good
for the world,—some do it with their society—some with their
wit—some with their benevolence—some with a sort of power

of conferring good humour on all they meet and in a thousand ways all equally dutiful to the command of Great Nature."

And because, herself a contemplative, she yet feels this lure and this worth in the life of action she communicates the tension between the two through the minds of the people she creates. Bernard, in *The Waves*, wishes:

"Once in a while to exercise my prerogative not always to act, but to explore; to hear vague ancestral sounds of boughs creaking, of mammoths, to indulge impossible desires to embrace the whole world with arms of understanding—impossible to those who act."

Yet Percival, the man of action, commands the love and veneration of the six characters in whose consciousness we live throughout *The Waves*, even though they know that they possess something he lacks. So Neville, a boy still at school, watches Percival going off to play cricket and reflects:

"He takes my devotion; he accepts my tremulous, no doubt abject offering, mixed with contempt as it is for his mind. For he cannot read. Yet when I read Shakespeare or Catullus, lying in the long grass, he understands more than Louis. Not the words—but what are words? Do I not know already how to rhyme, how to imitate Pope, Dryden, even Shakespeare? But I cannot stand all day in the sun with my eyes on the ball; I cannot feel the flight of the ball through my body and think only of the ball. I shall be a clinger to the outsides of words all my life. Yet I could not live with him and suffer his stupidity."

[*The Waves*]

And Bernard, when Percival is dead, sees to the root of what they all valued in him:

"Now, through my own infirmity I recover what he was to me: my opposite. Being naturally truthful, he did not see the point of these exaggerations, and was borne on by a natural sense

72

of the fitting, was indeed a great master of the art of living so
that he seems to have lived long, and to have spread calm round
him, indifference one might almost say, certainly to his own
advancement, save that he had also great compassion."

[*The Waves*]

Similarly Mrs Dalloway admires her husband's active concern
for the welfare of mankind; it is because he is capable of "doing
some good for the world...with his benevolence" that she
admires his "adorable, his divine simplicity which no one had
to the same extent; which made him go and do a thing while
she and Peter frittered their time away bickering".

In *The Voyage Out* Richard Dalloway's "simplicity" was
placed in a less sympathetic light. There he is felt to be vain
about his good works, he boasts of the benefits he has conferred
by his political activity, so that Rachel sets him on a pedestal
and then—notwithstanding his happiness with Clarissa—he cannot resist making love to her. In *The Voyage Out* the claim of
the active benefactors, the improvers of society, that they are
of more value than the poets, is presented with mockery. Richard
gives Rachel a brief homily on the subject:

"'Well, when I consider my life, there is one fact I admit that
I'm proud of; owing to me some thousands of girls in Lancashire—
and many thousands to come after them—can spend an hour
every day in the open air which their mothers had to spend over
their looms. I'm prouder of that, I own, than I should be of
writing Keats and Shelley into the bargain.'

"It became painful to Rachel to be one of those who write
Keats and Shelley."   [*The Voyage Out*]

She tries to explain to the politician her own different vision of
life, which is focused upon the isolated individual: "An old widow
in her room, somewhere, let us suppose, in the suburbs of Leeds."
And Rachel can imagine that, owing to Richard's parliamentary

speeches, the old widow may go to her cupboard and find a little more sugar or a little more tea.

"Still, there's the mind of the widow—the affections; those you leave untouched."
[*The Voyage Out*]

And Richard explains further, asking her to conceive of the state as a "complicated machine". But

"It was impossible to combine the image of a lean black widow, gazing out of her window, and longing for someone to talk to, with the image of a vast machine, such as one sees at South Kensington, thumping, thumping, thumping. The attempt at communication had been a failure."
[*The Voyage Out*]

This same failure of communication is treated with a deeper understanding, a fuller sympathy for the two participants in failure, in a posthumous short story, *The Man who Loved his Kind*. Prickett Ellis, barrister, pleads the case of two poor clients and asks no fee; he is deeply touched by their thankoffering: "That was what he worked for, that was his reward." The story introduces him to us at the Dalloways' party and he watches with hostility the complacent, fashionable world. The reader is made to enter into his mind and to understand his feeling. Yet there is a flaw:

"He did not feel this—that he loved humanity, that he paid only fivepence an ounce for tobacco and loved nature—naturally and quietly. Each of these pleasures had been turned into a protest. He felt that these people whom he despised made him stand and deliver and justify himself. 'I am an ordinary man', he kept saying. And what he said next he was really ashamed of saying, but he said it. 'I have done more for my kind in one day than the rest of you in all your lives.'"

[*A Haunted House*. The Hogarth Press, 1943.
The Man who Loved His Kind.]

Presently he is introduced to Miss O'Keefe, who is in a haughty and difficult mood because

"she had seen a woman and two children, very poor, very tired, pressing against the railings of a square, peering in, that hot afternoon. Can't they be let in? she had thought, her pity rising like a wave; her indignation boiling."

[*The Man who Loved His Kind*]

But these two lovers of their kind cannot find a common language. She talks of poetry, the arts, beauty for

"the root of things, what they were all afraid of saying, was that happiness is dirt cheap. You can have it for nothing. Beauty."

and he talks of his deeds: "Up at six; interviews; smelling a drain in a filthy slum; then to court." The few brief pages of the short story are enough to point to the gathering fog of misunderstanding until

"Hating each other, hating the whole houseful of people who had given them this painful, this disillusioning evening, these two lovers of their kind got up, and without a word parted for ever."

The creator of Prickett Ellis and Miss O'Keefe has understood them both. Moreover, here she has not weighted the balance against the active man by reducing (or enlarging) his activity to one that concerns a "complicated machine". Prickett Ellis is actively benevolent to individual human beings, while Miss O'Keefe merely contemplates them with pity and love. He has a stronger case to plead than she has, before the bar of the reader's intellect. But that, of course, is not the point. The story is not a parable from which a moral is to be drawn. It opens a window through which the reader can see into the heart of both characters, though neither can perceive the heart of the other. Virginia

Woolf herself, because for her "that one talent which 'tis death to hide" is the gift of artistic creation, is necessarily more nearly akin to the contemplative than to the active being.

It is observable that, in her novels, women of action, even those who embrace the Feminist Cause, are perceived as a little comic. Yet it is clear from *Three Guineas* and from *A Room of One's Own* that, outside the creative mood, Virginia Woolf believed in this cause. There is some oscillation in *Night and Day* between ridicule and admiration for Mrs Seal, the active feminist; the total effect is of amused sympathy, comparable to the final effect of Miss Bates in *Emma*. Mary Datchet certainly is both admirable and lovable; but then her activities are, in the main, palliatives for her private sorrows:

"Her old convictions had come back to her. But they had only come back, she thought with scorn at her feebleness, because she wanted to use them to fight against Ralph. They weren't, rightly speaking, convictions at all. She could not see the world divided into separate compartments of good people and bad people, any more than she could believe so implicitly in the rightness of her own thought as to wish to bring the population of the British Isles into agreement with it." [*Night and Day*]

In *The Years* again, Rose Pargiter, the militant suffragette, is presented with an admiration tempered by amusement.

Virginia Woolf's own contribution to the feminist cause is, in her creative work, something much more interesting and profound than an advocacy of equal rights. Writing as she does with unfaltering fidelity to her own vision, she unveils the essential quality of female experience where it differs from the male. She notes, of course, the wavering character of the dividing line, she sees the qualities of each sex appearing in the other. But she discerns more clearly perhaps than any other novelist the peculiar nature of typically feminine modes of thought and apprehension,

and their peculiar value as the complement of masculine modes.
Different women in her novels, women who are clearly distin-
guished from one another, share this essential womanliness. Mrs
Flanders has it and Mrs Ramsay, Mrs Dalloway and Eleanor
Pargiter; in *The Waves* we find it in Susan, in Rhoda and in
Jinny, although the three are so different, in *Between the Acts*
it is discernible in Mrs Manresa as well as in Mrs Swithin and
Mrs Giles Oliver. To isolate the feminine quality from the total
impression of the personality would be to falsify it. But an element in it is undeniably what the masculine mind would call
vagueness or even muddleheadedness. In its simplest form we
find it in *Jacob's Room*, a book in which the writer still preserves
the liberty of acting as commentator:

"'What did I ask you to remember?' she said.
"'I don't know', said Archer.
"'Well, I don't know either', said Betty, humorously and
simply, and who shall deny that this blankness of mind, when
combined with profusion, mother wit, old wives' tales, hap-
hazard ways, moments of astonishing daring, humour, and
sentimentality—who shall deny that in these respects every
woman is nicer than any man?"   [*Jacob's Room*]

Certainly an element in the typically feminine experience, as
Virginia Woolf sees it, is an incapacity for retaining, or distinguishing between, facts. Mrs Dalloway can never remember
whether her husband's concern is for Armenians or for Albanians.
Mr Ramsay, talking to his daughter Cam, reflects upon the
vagueness of women's minds; seeing her in the boat gazing about
her:

"he began to tease her. Didn't she know the points of the
compass? he asked. Didn't she know the North from the South?
Did she really think they lived right out there? And he pointed
again and showed her where their house was, there, by those

trees. He wished she would try to be more accurate, he said: 'Tell me—which is East, which is West?' he said, half laughing at her, half scolding her, for he could not understand the state of mind of any one, not absolutely imbecile, who did not know the points of the compass. Yet she did not know. And seeing her gazing, with her vague, now rather frightened eyes fixed where no house was....He thought, women are always like that; the vagueness of their minds is hopeless; it was a thing he had never been able to understand; but so it was. It had been so with her—his wife. They could not keep anything clearly fixed in their minds." [To the Lighthouse]

The reader knows, as Mr Ramsay does not, of what Cam was actually thinking when she gazed vacantly in the wrong direction. She was thinking not of the geographical facts about the position of the house, but of the truth about its existence:

"She was thinking how all those paths and the lawn, thick and knotted with the lives they had lived there, were gone: were rubbed out; were past; were unreal, and now this was real; the boat and the sail with its patch; Macalister with his earrings; the noise of the waves—all this was real." [To the Lighthouse]

Just as Mr Ramsay cannot understand the feminine mind, so is Mrs Ramsay perplexed by the masculine. But there is a difference —characteristic both of her and of her sex—she perceives its value clearly, she respects it immensely: Mrs Ramsay listens to what her husband is saying at the other end of the table about

"the square root of one thousand two hundred and fifty three, which happened to be the number on his railway ticket.

"What did it all mean? To this day she had no notion. A square root? What was that? Her sons knew. She leant on them; on cubes and square roots; that was what they were talking about now; on Voltaire and Madame de Staël; on the character of Napoleon; on the French system of land tenure; on Lord Rosebery; on Creevey's Memoires: she let it uphold her and sustain her, this admirable fabric of the masculine intelligence, which ran up and down, crossed this way and that, like iron girders spanning the swaying fabric, upholding the world, so that she could trust herself to it utterly, even shut her eyes, or flicker them for a moment, as a child staring up from its pillow winks at the myriad layers of the leaves of a tree. Then she woke up. It was still being fabricated. William Bankes was praising the Waverley novels."

[To the Lighthouse]

Possibly Virginia Woolf's own inaccuracy in matters of fact is due to the essential feminineness of her mind. Or perhaps it is a deliberate carelessness about all that is not essential to her vision. It has been pointed out that her flowers bloom at impossible times and in impossible places; that her champagne bottles can be opened with corkscrews, that Claridges stands where no Londoner has ever found it. Those whom these vagaries leave unmoved, may wince when Orlando reads Sir Thomas Browne in the reign of Queen Elizabeth, or when Mrs Dalloway admires the character of Clytemnestra in the *Antigone*. Virginia Woolf is indifferent to fact:

"Desiring truth, awaiting it, laboriously distilling a few words, for ever desiring—."

[*Monday or Tuesday.*]

The truth she desires above all is the truth about individual human beings, so unlike is it, as she knows, to the phrases we make about them. A little story in *The Haunted House*[1] points to the difference between truth and fact, and between the reality and what we invent about each other. The reader listens to the reflections of one character seeking to define another, Isabella Tyson, whom she has known for many years:

"She suggested the fantastic and the tremulous convolvulus rather than the upright aster, the starched zinnia, or her own burning roses alight like lamps on the straight posts of their

1 *The Lady in the Looking-Glass.*

rose trees. The comparison showed how very little, after all these years, one knew about her; for it is impossible that any woman of flesh and blood of fifty-five or sixty should be really a wreath or a tendril. Such comparisons are worse than idle and super-ficial—they are cruel even, for they come like the convolvulus itself trembling between one's eyes and the truth. There must be truth; there must be a wall. Yet it was strange that after knowing her all these years one could not say what the truth about Isabella was; one still made up phrases like this about convolvulus and travellers' joy. As for facts, it was a fact that she was a spinster; that she was rich; that she had bought this house...."

[*The Lady in the Looking-Glass*]

The argument in *Mr Bennett and Mrs Brown* concerns this same difference between fact and truth. Mr Galsworthy, Mr Wells and Mr Bennett, she observes, note the facts about the shabbily dressed little woman in the corner of the railway carriage. They relate them to other facts about the social and economic environ-ment, but the truth about her life and her being they do not approach. In *An Unwritten Novel*, a short story in the posthumous volume, she applies her own method to a similar figure, and exposes the elusiveness of what she seeks; for whereas the face suggests the story of a lonely, embittered spinster, the owner of it is met at the station by an attentive son. Facts may deceive; even such facts as that

"Such an expression of unhappiness was enough by itself to make one's eyes slide above the paper's edge to the poor woman's face—insignificant without that look, almost a symbol of human destiny with it."

[*An Unwritten Novel*]

If, as Virginia Woolf sees it, the typically feminine mind lacks the sense of fact, what has it in compensation, and by what virtue can it complement the typically masculine mind? First of all, at its best, it has an especial honesty, an honesty which comes of self-knowledge, and the power of distinguishing the essential from the accidental. Mrs Ramsay is more honest than her husband. He can be deflected from the truth by vanity, by egotism, even by the distasteful recognition of facts which seem irreconcilable:

"If Shakespeare had never existed, he asked, would the world have differed much from what it is to-day? Does the progress of civilization depend upon great men? Is the lot of the average human being better now than in the time of the Pharaohs? Is the lot of the average human being, however, he asked himself, the criterion by which we judge the measure of civilization? Possibly not. Possibly the greatest good requires the existence of a slave class. The liftman in the Tube is an eternal necessity. The thought was distasteful to him. He tossed his head. To avoid it, he would find some way of snubbing the predominance of the arts. He would argue that the world exists for the average human being; that the arts are merely a decoration imposed on the top of human life; they do not express it. Nor is Shakespeare necessary to it. Not knowing precisely why he wanted to disparage Shakespeare and come to the rescue of the man who stands eternally at the door of the lift, he picked a leaf sharply from the hedge."   [*To the Lighthouse*]

Mr Ramsay, lacking "the power of being in uncertainties without irritably seeking after the fact", denies a truth because two facts—or perhaps only two meanings of a word—seem to conflict. But Mrs Ramsay will not lie to herself. Sitting looking at the light flashing from the lighthouse, she reflects:

"Often she found herself sitting and looking, sitting and looking, with her work in her hands until she became the thing she looked at—that light for example. And it would lift up on it some little phrase or other which had been lying in her mind like that—'children don't forget, children don't forget'—which she would repeat and begin adding to it, It will end, It will end, she said. It will come, it will come, when suddenly she added, We are in the hands of the Lord.

"But instantly she was annoyed with herself for saying that. Who had said it? not she; she had been trapped into saying something she did not mean. She looked up over her knitting and met the third stroke and it seemed to her like her own eyes meeting her own eyes, searching as she alone could search into her mind and her heart, purifying out of existence that lie, any lie. She praised herself in praising the light, without vanity, for she was stern, she was searching, she was beautiful like that light....

"What brought her to say that: 'We are in the hands of the Lord?' she wondered. The insincerity slipping in among the truths roused her, annoyed her. She returned to her knitting again. How could any Lord have made this world? she asked. With her mind she had always seized the fact that there is no reason, order, justice: but suffering, death, the poor."

[*To the Lighthouse*]

Mrs Ramsay and Mr Ramsay are alike distressed by the injustice they discern in the world, but he, because it is unjust that the high achievement of the mind should flower out of a society that is based on servitude, denies the value of that achievement. He lies to himself about it. It is she who insists upon facing the truth. For Lucy Swithin (in *Between the Acts*) the truth includes a God and for all her brother's mockery she speaks as she feels:

"'It's very unsettled. It'll rain, I'm afraid. We can only pray', she added, and fingered her crucifix.

"'And provide umbrellas', said her brother.

"Lucy flushed. He had struck at her faith. When she said 'pray', he added 'umbrellas'. She half covered the cross with her fingers. She shrank; she cowered; but next moment she exclaimed:

"'Oh there they are—the darlings!'

"The perambulator was passing across the lawn.

"Isa looked too. What an angel she was—the old woman! Thus to salute the children; to beat up against those immensities and the old man's irreverencies her skinny hands, her laughing eyes! How courageous to defy Bart and the weather."

[*Between the Acts*]

Integrity and courage are among the gifts with which Virginia Woolf endows her women, for Lucy Swithin is another of those who are peculiarly feminine. Bart her brother thinks about her:

"She would have been, he thought, a very clever woman, had she fixed her gaze. But this led to that; that to the other. What went in at this ear, went out at that." [*Between the Acts*]

And he loves her, but laughs at her:

"'Superstition', he said.
"She flushed, and the little breath too was audible that she drew in as once more he struck a blow at her faith. But, brother and sister, flesh and blood was not a barrier but a mist. Nothing changed their affection; no argument; no fact; no truth. What she saw he didn't—and so on, *ad infinitum*." [*Between the Acts*]

When there is love between a man and a woman—and no novelist has understood this condition of things more fully than Virginia Woolf—the differences between them become contributory to a whole, as though together they made up a human being more complete than either. So it is with Lucy and her brother, with Clarissa and Richard Dalloway, with Mr and Mrs Hilbery, with Mr and Mrs Ramsay.

Throughout the day that occupies the first movement of *To the Lighthouse* the reader gradually discovers the relation between Mr and Mrs Ramsay. We see them together and apart, reflected in other minds and reflected in each other's. Mrs Ramsay soothes his wounded vanity, fosters his faith in himself. Mr Ramsay gives her a sense of security, of stability and of confidence in life. In the evening we see them alone together. She reflects about his vanity, his concern for his own fame, and it distresses her lest any one else should notice this flaw in him:

"It didn't matter, any of it, she thought. A great man, a great book, fame—who could tell? She knew nothing about it. But

it was his way with him, his truthfulness—for instance at dinner she had been thinking quite instinctively, If only he would speak! She had complete trust in him."
[To the Lighthouse]

Now he is reading Scott, and she is reading poetry:

"Until a little sound roused her—her husband slapping his thighs. Their eyes met for a second; but they did not want to speak to each other. They had nothing to say, but something seemed, nevertheless, to go from him to her. It was the life, it was the power of it, it was the tremendous humour, she knew, that made him slap his thighs. Don't interrupt me, he seemed to be saying, don't say anything; just sit there."
[To the Lighthouse]

He forgets himself in his joyful recognition of the greatness of the novel. But he had turned to it because of something Mr Tansley had said, about people not reading Scott any more; that had made him think "That's what they'll say of me". Now the thought returns:

"One ought not to complain, thought Mr Ramsay, trying to stifle his desire to complain to his wife that young men did not admire him. But he was determined; he would not bother her again. Here he looked at her reading. She looked very peaceful, reading. He liked to think that every one had taken themselves off and that he and she were alone."
[To the Lighthouse]

And each goes on reading, Scott purges away his vanity and the poem satisfies a need in her:

"All the odds and ends of the day stuck to this magnet; her mind felt swept, felt clean. And then there it was, suddenly entire shaped in her hands beautiful and reasonable, clear and complete, the essence sucked out of life and held rounded here—the sonnet."
[To the Lighthouse]

Mr Ramsay looks at her, dozing over her book, as he believes:

84

"And he wondered what she was reading, and exaggerated her ignorance, her simplicity, for he liked to think that she was not clever, not book-learned at all. He wondered if she understood what she was reading. Probably not, he thought. She was astonishingly beautiful."

[*To the Lighthouse*]

Mrs Ramsay looks up from her book; she can feel that now he wants to talk with her, she thinks of the day and all that has passed and she speaks of the engagement of Paul and Minta:

"'They're engaged', she said, beginning to knit, 'Paul and Minta.'

"'So I guessed', he said."

[*To the Lighthouse*]

And for a while they sit silent, each still half absorbed in what they have been reading:

"Then she became aware that she wanted him to say something....Slowly it came into her head, why is it then that one wants people to marry? What was the value, the meaning of things? (Every word they said now would be true.) Do say something she thought, wishing only to hear his voice. For the shadow, the thing folding them in was beginning, she felt, to close round her again. Say anything, she begged; looking at him, as if for help.

"He was silent, swinging the compass on his watch chain to and fro, and thinking of Scott's novels and Balzac's novels. But through the crepuscular walls of their intimacy, for they were drawing together, involuntarily, coming side by side, quite close, she could feel his mind like a raised hand shadowing her mind; and he was beginning now that her thoughts took a turn he disliked—towards this 'pessimism' as he called it—to fidget, though he said nothing, raising his hand to his forehead, twisting a lock of hair, letting it fall again.

"'You won't finish that stocking to-night', he said, pointing to her stocking. That was what she wanted—the asperity in his voice reproving her. If he says it's wrong to be pessimistic probably it is wrong, she thought; the marriage will turn out all right."

[*To the Lighthouse*]

And as they sit and talk, not saying much in words, intimacy deepens and the love of each for the other. He would like her to put it into words:

"But she could not do it; she could not say it. Then, knowing that he was watching her, instead of saying anything she turned, holding her stocking, and looked at him. And as she looked at him she began to smile, for though she had not said a word, he knew, of course he knew, that she loved him. He could not deny it. And smiling she looked out of the window and said (thinking to herself, Nothing on earth can equal this happiness)—

"'Yes, you were right. It's going to be wet tomorrow.' She had not said it, but he knew it." [*To the Lighthouse*]

Almost precisely the same words express the thought of Richard Dalloway when he too has found a way, without words, of telling Clarissa that he loves her:

"(But he could not tell her he loved her. He held her hand. Happiness is this, he thought.)" [*Mrs Dalloway*]

When the reader looks back over the novels it is clear that, although the "philosophy" has been "consumed" and he cannot "underline this phrase" or "cut out that exhortation", yet there are positives and there are negatives, things that the writer has made us admire, and things from which she has made us recoil. We have admired the mutual forbearance and respect which keep love untarnished in spite of temperamental differences. And we have admired disinterestedness, Mr Bankes, for instance, who can praise what seems good to him without thought of himself, rather than Mr Tansley who

"wanted to assert himself, and so it would always be with him till he got his Professorship or married his wife, and so need not be always saying, 'I—I—I'. For that is what his criticism of poor Sir Walter or perhaps it was Jane Austen, amounted to. 'I—I—I.' He was thinking of himself and the impression he was making, as she could tell by the sound of his voice, and his emphasis and his uneasiness. Success would be good for him."

[To the Lighthouse]

But Mr Bankes can say:

"'Let us enjoy what we do enjoy.'...His integrity seemed to Mrs Ramsay quite admirable. He never seemed for a moment to think, But how does this affect me?" *[To the Lighthouse]*

And when Mrs Ramsay herself, in the light of Mr Carmichael's appraising eye, suspects the purity of her own motives, it is this same disinterestedness that she covets:

"For her own self-satisfaction was it that she wished so instinctively to help, to give, that people might say of her, 'O Mrs Ramsay! dear Mrs Ramsay...Mrs Ramsay, of course' and need her and send for her and admire her? Was it not secretly this that she wanted, and therefore when Mr Carmichael shrank away from her, as he did at this moment...she did not feel merely snubbed back in her instinct, but made aware of the pettiness of some part of her, and of human relations, how flawed they are, how despicable, how self-seeking, at their best."

[To the Lighthouse]

And Clarissa Dalloway has a precisely similar thought:

"How much she wanted it—that people should look pleased as she came in, Clarissa thought and turned and walked back towards Bond Street, annoyed, because it was silly to have other reasons for doing things." *[Mrs Dalloway]*

We then have been led to admire integrity, and also courage such as Mrs Swithin has, or such as Clarissa thinks of as she reads

"in the book spread open:

> Fear no more the heat o' the sun
> Nor the furious winter's rages.

This late age of the world's experience had bred in them all,

all men and women, a well of tears. Tears and sorrows; courage and endurance; a perfectly upright and stoical bearing."

[*Mrs Dalloway*]

Or the courage of Jinny in *The Waves*, Jinny who has lived to the full the life of the senses, the life offered to her by her innate power to attract and who, in middle age, recognizes that those powers are waning:

"'Here I stand', said Jinny, 'in the Tube station where everything that is desirable meets—Piccadilly South Side, Piccadilly North Side, Regent Street and the Haymarket. I stand for a moment under the pavement in the heart of London. Innumerable wheels rush and feet press just over my head. The great avenues of civilisation meet here and strike this way and that. I am in the heart of life. But look—there is my body in that looking glass. How solitary, how shrunk, how aged! I am no longer young. I am no longer part of the procession. Millions descend those stairs in a terrible descent. Great wheels churn inexorably urging them downwards. Millions have died. Percival died. I still move. I still live. But who will come if I signal.

"'Little animal that I am, sucking my flanks in and out with fear, I stand here, palpitating, trembling. But I will not be afraid. I will bring the whip down on my flanks. I am not a whimpering little animal making for the shadow. It was only for a moment, catching sight of myself before I had time to prepare myself as I always prepare myself for the sight of myself, that I quailed. It is true; I am not young—I shall soon raise my arm in vain and my scarf will fall to my side without having signalled. I shall not hear the sudden sigh in the night and feel through the dark someone coming. There will be no reflections in window panes in dark tunnels. I shall look into faces, and I shall see them seek some other face. I admit, for one moment the soundless flight of upright bodies down the moving stairs like the pinioned and terrible descent of some army of the dead downwards and the churning of the great engines remorselessly forwarding us, all of us, onward made me cower and run for shelter.

"'But now I swear, making deliberately in front of the glass those slight preparations that equip me, I will not be afraid. Think of the superb omnibuses, red and yellow, stopping and starting, punctually in order. Think of the powerful and beautiful cars that now slow to a foot's pace and now shoot forward; think of men, think of women, equipped, prepared, driving onward. This is the triumphant procession; this is the army of victory with banners and brass eagles and heads crowned with laurel-leaves won in battle. They are better than savages in loin-cloths, and women whose hair is dank, whose long breasts sag, with children tugging at their long breasts. These broad thoroughfares—Piccadilly South, Piccadilly North, Regent Street and the Haymarket— are sanded paths of victory driven through the jungle. I too, with my little patent leather shoes, my handkerchief that is but a film of gauze, my reddened lips and my finely pencilled eyebrows, march to victory with the band.'"

[*The Waves*]

And, besides integrity, and courage, we have admired compassion, the manly compassion that redeems the stupidity of Percival, or the womanly compassion that perceives even the least spectacular human pain and instinctively relieves it. This is the quality that causes Mrs Swithin to take William Dodge to see the house with her and that he recognizes and reverences:

"Old and frail she had climbed these stairs. She had spoken her thoughts, ignoring, not caring if he thought her, as he had, inconsequent, sentimental, foolish. She had lent him a hand to help him up a steep place. She had guessed his trouble."

[*Between the Acts*]

A clear, fastidious, impassioned sense of values has replaced, in Virginia Woolf's novels, the "palpable design" of the moralist. In *The Waves*, where the reader lives solely within the minds of the characters, seeing the world through their eyes, from youth to age, there is no moment at which the writer can deduce or conclude or by any means announce her own opinion. But she

89

has necessarily chosen six personalities in whose vision of the world she participates. So full and subtle a record of experience would not otherwise be possible. Despite their differences of temperament and of desire, the six share, each in their measure, her own sense of values. Above all they share an integrity of purpose which gives them the power to discover the principle of their own nature and to live (or, in Rhoda's case, to die) in a courageous, disinterested endeavour to fulfil it.

CHAPTER V

THE FORM OF THE NOVELS

Virginia Woolf, in her essay on *Mr Bennett and Mrs Brown* in 1924, affirmed that the Edwardian novelists had

"made tools and established conventions which do their business; and that business is not our business. For us those conventions are ruin, those tools death."

Her own continual experiments with the form of the novel were the consequence of that belief. What then did she feel to be her "business" as a novelist? To say that it was to communicate human experience is not enough; for the same might be said of all serious novelists. What she most clearly knew that she wanted to do was to record what life felt like to living beings. This was also what Dorothy Richardson had discovered in 1913 that she wished to do, and she shows us, with fine perception, through a long and leisurely progress, what life felt like to Miriam. But Virginia Woolf was not content with the record of a single mind. She wanted also to communicate the impression made by one individual upon others and to reveal human personality partly through its own self-consciousness and partly through the picture projected by it upon other minds. This was the starting point which impelled her to break away from the tradition, in *Jacob's Room*. There she makes her first attempt to remove the narrator from the scene, so that the reader may seem to see the subject solely through the eyes of the people in the book. But elimination is not yet completely effected. There are passages of description, events are recorded, comments are made not by the characters themselves but by their author:

"Elizabeth Flanders, of whom this and much more than this had been said and would be said, was, of course, a widow in her prime. She was half-way between forty and fifty."

[*Jacob's Room*]

Later such necessary facts will be given through the reflection of some other mind in the book, not from without; Mrs Dalloway's age and appearance for instance:

"A charming woman, Scrope Purvis thought her (knowing her as one does know people who live next door to one in Westminster); a touch of the bird about her, of the jay, blue-green, light, vivacious, though she was over fifty, and grown very white since her illness. There she perched, never seeing him, waiting to cross, very upright."

[*Mrs Dalloway*]

Nor is it only description and the record of event that brings the narrator forward in *Jacob's Room*—she is still, like her forerunners, though less continuously, present as commentator:

"Anyhow, whether undergraduate or shop boy, man or woman, it must come as a shock about the age of twenty—the world of the elderly—thrown up in such black outline upon what we are; upon the reality; the moors and Byron, the sea and the lighthouse; the sheep's jaw with the yellow teeth in it; upon the obstinate irrepressible conviction which makes youth so intolerably disagreeable—'I am what I am, and intend to be it', for which there will be no form in the world unless Jacob makes one for himself."

[*Jacob's Room*]

But the direction, in which already she is moving, is towards complete objectivity, not the objectivity of drama, which is limited to the enacted scene and the spoken word, but an objectivity in which the feelings, the meditations, the memories of the protagonists are projected, without intervention upon the mind of the reader. When James in *To the Lighthouse* emerges into manhood, we receive his impressions of "the world of the elderly", linked as Jacob's are with past memories and with projects for the future, through the medium of his own reflections:

"He had always kept this old symbol of taking a knife and striking his father to the heart. Only now, as he grew older, and sat staring at his father in an impotent rage, it was not him, that old man reading, whom he wanted to kill, but it was the thing that descended on him—without his knowing it perhaps: that fierce sudden black-winged harpy, with its talons and its beak all cold and hard, that struck and struck at you (he could feel the beak on his bare legs, where it had struck him when a child) and then made off, and there he was again, an old man, very sad, reading his book. That he would kill, that he would strike to the heart. Whatever he did—(and he might do anything, he felt, looking at the Lighthouse and the distant shore) whether he was in business, in a bank, a barrister, a man at the head of some enterprise, that he would fight, that he would track down and stamp out—tyranny, despotism, he called it—making people do what they did not want to do, cutting off their right to speak."

[To the Lighthouse]

And just as the passage about Jacob throws the reader's mind back to an earlier scene in which the sheep's jaw figured as the token of his childish self-assertion, so here, but with a richer complexity, James's meditations and the images in which he frames them, recall an earlier scene in which the demanding, uncomprehending figure of his father strode between the little boy and his mother:

"At the window he bent quizzically and whimsically to tickle James's bare calf with a sprig of something, she twitted him for having despatched 'that poor young man', Charles Tansley. Tansley had had to go in and write his dissertation, he said.

"'James will have to write *his* dissertation one of these days', he added ironically, flicking his sprig.

"Hating his father, James brushed away the tickling spray with which in a manner peculiar to him, compound of severity and humour, he teased his youngest son's bare leg." *[To the Lighthouse]*

The will to discover and record life as it feels to those who live it was the originating cause of Virginia Woolf's rejection of existing conventions. It was this primarily that impelled her to eliminate narration and comment. In *Jacob's Room*, however, certain needs arising out of her vision of the subject prevented her from achieving that purpose. She had yet to learn how to communicate all the facts that need to be known, how to mark the passage of time, how to indicate the point of view, without speaking in her own person. In this first experiment she is avowedly conscious of her difficulties and has not learnt the art to conceal her art. Thus she will recount Jacob's words, thoughts, acts and then—much as Fielding used to do—she will insert an essay upon the art of fiction:

But though all this may very well be true—so Jacob thought and spoke—so he crossed his legs—filled his pipe—sipped his whisky, and once looked at his pocket-book, rumpling his hair as he did so, there remains over something which can never be conveyed to a second person save by Jacob himself. Moreover, part of this is not Jacob but Richard Bonamy—the room; the market carts; the hour; the very moment of history. Then consider the effect of sex—how between man and woman it hangs wavy, tremulous, so that here's a valley, there's a peak, when in truth, perhaps, all's as flat as my hand. Even the exact words get the wrong accent on them. But something is always impelling one to hum vibrating, like the hawk moth, at the mouth of the cavern of mystery, endowing Jacob Flanders with all sorts of qualities he had not at all—for though, certainly, he sat talking to Bonamy, half of what he said was too dull to repeat; much unintelligible (about unknown people and Parliament); what remains is mostly a matter of guesswork. Yet over him we hang vibrating. [*Jacob's Room*]

The essay interrupts the illusion; but it is an invaluable document, for it enumerates the difficulties which, later, her craftsmanship was to overcome. Presently she would devise a form whereby she could communicate directly that "something which remains over" and can only be conveyed by Jacob himself, a form whereby, also, she could indicate the degree in which, at any given moment, a personality is not itself merely, but an instrument played upon by another and affected by the room, the street, the hour and "the very moment of history". She learnt to impart directly "the effect of sex", and to communicate the mysterious complexity of living experience.

Jacob's Room, because no adequate substitute has been devised to replace the old conventions, falls apart. The reader is left with the impression of a series of episodes, each of them conveyed with depth and subtlety, so that at each successive moment he is vividly aware of how life felt to Jacob, or of how Jacob affected some other. But the successive moments build up no whole that can be held in the mind. In the traditional novel the episodes are interwoven to compose a story. In that story one character is central and stands in some significant relation to the other characters and their stories. So, for instance, the story of Emma is interwoven with the story of Jane Fairfax and with the story of Harriet Smith; every other character in the book plays some part in those stories and the combined effect of all is to illuminate the central character. When the reader closes the book he has a complete pattern in his mind, the pattern by which Emma's emerging self-knowledge has been communicated. To that emergence each of the other characters was contributory and Jane Austen selected the episodes so that they might effect it. The episodes of which *Jacob's Room* is composed are chosen to reveal the impact of Jacob's developing personality upon the people with whom he comes into contact and, to a lesser degree, the impact of the external world and of other people upon Jacob. It must be of set purpose that we are given more of Jacob's reflection in other minds than of his own experience. But the result is that Jacob remains a nebulous young man, indeed almost any young man, and the reader does not fully participate in the powerful effect he makes upon others. Moreover, in so far as the writer has succeeded in effacing herself, the people she creates have to take her place. Their consciousness of the world and the people in it must be made adequate to communicate all that the writer requires the reader to know and to feel. Consequently a number of persons become momentarily very prominent. The effect is much as it would be if most of the characters in *Hamlet* were given monologues as soul-searching as the prince's own. From moment to moment, while they hold the stage, the reader is fascinated and deeply attentive. But ultimately his attention is dissipated and diffused. Too many disassociated, or only tenuously related, demands have been made upon it. A similar effect is produced by a later, and, in many ways, greater book than *Jacob's Room, The Years*. By the time Virginia Woolf wrote this, she had developed her own method of presentation very fully, although the scale upon which the book is planned, spanning nearly sixty years and tracing the life-course of two generations, necessitates an element of narration. It is, however, reduced to a minimum, and the reader is continually aware of such facts as the season, the weather, the place as reflected in some human consciousness.

"But in April such weather was to be expected. Thousands of shop assistants made that remark as they handed neat parcels to ladies in flounced dresses standing on the other side of the counter of Whiteley's and the Army and Navy Stores. Interminable processions of shoppers in the West End, of business men in the East, paraded the pavements, like caravans perpetually marching,—so it seemed to those who had any reason to pause, say, to post a letter, or at a club window in Piccadilly."

[*The Years*]

More subtle and complex reflections are given through a particular consciousness, and it is the number of people whom we are invited to know with this degree of intimacy that obscures the pattern of the whole. When a novelist uses the older convention of narrative and characterization a large number of characters living through a long stretch of time can be more easily united. The stories and the groups of characters in, for instance, *Middlemarch* are all related in a number of ways to the story of Dorothea. The pattern of each story can be recalled in isolation and can readily be re-incorporated into the pattern of the whole. Minor characters are kept, by the novelist, in due subordination to major characters; neither the events of their lives nor their experience of living are given prominence. The new method deepens the reader's intimacy with the persons in the book at the risk, if there are many of them, of impeding his width of view. He cannot see the wood for the trees. The trees are magnificent, and one returns to them again and again with renewed pleasure, Eleanor, Kitty, Edward, Maggie and Sara (especially Sara), Rose, Martin, Morris and then the younger generation, Peggy and North, each name calls to mind vivid moments of experience and luminously distinct personalities. But what remains in the mind is a series of episodes rather than parts of a whole. The episodes illustrate the passage of time and the diversity of the human scene, and they evoke reflection upon the changing climate of opinion in sixty years, and upon the impress of historical happenings in an individual consciousness. All this *The Years* can give while preserving the illusion that it is all received by the reader directly, without the intervention of the author. But the reader feels, as Miss La Trobe in *Between the Acts* fears her audience will do when she allows the unselected impressions of the present moment to take the place of her invented pageant:

"something was going wrong with the experiment. 'Reality too strong', she muttered."

[*Between the Acts*]

The total effect of *The Years* is too much like life itself; consummate though the art is with which the parts are constructed, too little has been done to construct the whole; the book shares in the uncoordinated character of normal experience.

This does not mean that Virginia Woolf's art is incapable of communicating experience that is wide as well as deep. But to do so she had to invent conventions as rigid or more rigid than the old ones that she discards. This she does in her four most satisfying novels, *Mrs Dalloway*, *To the Lighthouse*, *The Waves* and *Between the Acts*. There are certain resemblances between them in structure and in style. In each case a small group of people is selected, and through their closely interrelated experience the reader receives his total impression. In each case also certain images, phrases and symbols bind the whole together. Apart from these general resemblances each of these novels is a fresh attempt to solve the problems raised by the departure from traditional conventions. Her first problem is to preserve the illusion of direct contact with human beings in the process of immediate and random experience, while in fact so selecting that experience that it will form an ordered whole. Moreover, the totality aimed at, a whole that reflects human consciousness, must include not only the impressions made by physical surroundings and by other human beings but also the threefold effect of time; the passing moments or hours; the voyage from youth to age; and the historic time, or time in relation to nation-wide and world-wide event.

Three years after *Jacob's Room*, in 1925, *Mrs Dalloway* was published. The subject is similar in so far as the principal theme is one personality, affecting and affected by the others who come into contact with it. But in the later book the composition of the whole is superbly successful. The impression made upon the reader by the central personality is clear and full, whilst a far deeper and wider understanding of the surrounding lives is given than was achieved in *Jacob's Room*. The incidents or episodes are themselves even more vivid, but they cohere firmly together and finally leave an impression of unity. In *Mrs Dalloway* a convention or art form has been evolved which is more than adequate to take the place of the older convention of narrative and characterization. The necessary circumscription is imposed by the narrow framework of time; the whole of the action takes place within one day. It moves between Mrs Dalloway's preparation for her party in the morning and her presiding over it in the evening of the same day. Within this narrow frame, by means of the contacts she makes and the memories they evoke in her and in others, her life story from girlhood to her present age of fifty is gradually unfolded. The story of Septimus Warren Smith, who impinges upon her consciousness early in the day and whose death throws a shadow over her party in the evening, is the means of introducing another group of characters, a darker side of life, and a more profound sense of the historic background against which the whole is set. The major characters are no more than five and they stand out from the rest with a distinctive prominence, for it is they alone who reveal their thoughts to the reader in prolonged and repeated soliloquy as well as in conversation. These five major characters move round each other, as it were, in two concentric circles, Clarissa, Peter Walsh and (rather more faintly drawn) Richard Dalloway in the one, Septimus and Rezia Warren Smith in the other. Around each of these two inner circles there is a ring of minor characters such as Sally Seton, Lady Bruton, Hugh Whitbread, Elizabeth Dalloway and, that important foil to Clarissa, Doris Kilman: round the Warren Smith orbit move Dr Holmes and Sir William Bradshaw through whose appearance at the party the two themes are ultimately interlocked. Further in the background are a number of figures, unimportant in themselves, but helping to compose the total scene and each one of them supplying an essential part of the pattern.

But there is another point of view from which the subject of the book no longer appears to be the life story of Clarissa Dalloway, nor of Septimus Warren Smith, but human life itself, its tension between misery and happiness and its inevitable consummation in death. From this point of view the fabric of the book is spun between the lines

> "Fear no more the heat o' the sun
>> Nor the furious winter's rages;"

and

>> "If it were now to die
> 'Twere now to be most happy;"

lines from Shakespeare which are woven into Clarissa's reflections or those of Septimus unobtrusively, but which evoke their own poetic context and associations. For within the book there is a poetic pattern, probing to that deeper level at which the mind apprehends timeless values, as well as the prose pattern wherein the reader is given a picture of the modern world with its destructive forces of class-struggle, economic insecurity and war. On the prose plane there are the satiric portraits of the self-made, successful, impermeable nerve specialist (the most cruel and brilliant satiric portrait Virginia Woolf ever drew) and, hardly less harsh, the picture of the neurotic, self-tormenting, embittered governess. On this plane too is one aspect of Septimus, the sympathetic yet slightly mocking account of his intellectual aspirations and romantic notions before war shattered him and, at the same time, lifted him on to the plane of tragedy. On that poetic plane there are only love and death and the evanescent beauty of the world.

From now on Virginia Woolf planned all her books, with the exception of *The Years*, within a narrow framework. She achieved this either by confining the action to a brief period of time, or by limiting the foreground characters to a small number, or by employing both these devices. Despite the narrow area of time within which the story usually moves, she yet contrives to give the reader an intimate knowledge of much that has preceded the action. In this her art is comparable with Ibsen's who, while keeping his drama within the unities of time and place can so draw upon his characters' memories as to unfold for the audience all that is relevant in their past histories. In *To the Lighthouse* the outward structure is simple. It consists of three movements of unequal length and of two different kinds, as it were two acts linked by a chorus. The first and longest act covers less than one day and is framed between Mrs Ramsay's opening words: "Yes, of course, if its fine tomorrow,"—that is, if it's fine we shall go to the lighthouse—and, the last words spoken by her in the book, "Yes, you were right, its going to be wet tomorrow." After this there follows, as it were, a choral ode which marks the passage of ten years. It is framed between the close of the day recorded in the first movement and Lily Briscoe's awakening ten years later, back once more in the Ramsays' house after Mrs Ramsay's death. The third act again covers less than a day and is enclosed between Lily's morning reflections: "What does it mean, what can it all mean?" and her evening reflections, as she finishes that picture which she began ten years ago and says: "I have had my vision." Only ten characters make any prominent appearance and of those ten only seven, Mr and Mrs Ramsay, Lily, Mr Bankes, Mr Tansley, James and Cam reveal themselves fully in speech and in soliloquy.

As in *Mrs Dalloway*, the form is the vehicle for two kinds of experience one on the plane of prose and the other on the plane of poetry. The double effect is analogous to that of the greatest poetic drama, and to some kinds of lyric poetry, in which the surface statement has, as it were, folded within in it, the poetic meaning. The surface statement can be summarized or defined while the other can only be suggested, since it depends upon the thoughts and feelings evoked by imagery and rhythm and these will be different for different readers and at different times. Similarly, Virginia Woolf's novels convey two different kinds of meaning to each of which the form is beautifully adapted.

On the prose plane *To the Lighthouse* tells about the Ramsay family, their relations to one another and to a small representative group of their friends. The visit to the lighthouse, projected and then frustrated by the weather in the first movement, and effected in the last, is an instrument to reveal certain aspects of character such as Mrs Ramsay's sympathetic understanding of other people's feelings, in particular those of her son James, Mr Ramsay's insensibility and his ruthless employment of logic and a sense of fact, Mr Tansley's aggressive self-assertiveness. The expedition provides an instance in relation to which the reader discerns Mr Ramsay's habitual insensitiveness to other people's feelings, it is remembered in the last movement, when, with Cam and James, he actually goes to the lighthouse, as the type of event in the past out of which the character of the boy has been formed. On this plane the reader's interest is centred in human character. The group of people assembled at the Ramsays' house, the Ramsays' children and friends, are all revealed in the light of their relation to Mrs Ramsay and to one another, both before and after her death. Mr Bankes's disinterested devotion to her physical and moral beauty, like his disinterested scientific curiosity, is a foil to Mr Ramsay's more self-regarding love and learning. Mr Tansley's sense of inferiority and consequent aggressiveness are brought out by his introduction, as Mr Ramsay's disciple, into a house-party to which he feels himself socially inferior and intellectually superior. Looked at from this point of view Lily Briscoe's endeavour to paint a picture of Mrs Ramsay, sitting on the steps of the house, and her subsequent completion of the picture is the expression of her sense of Mrs Ramsay's power to create order and harmony out of human relations. The manner in which the characters are presented, partly through their actions and conversation and partly through their own reflections, effects a happy combination of amused appraisal with sympathetic understanding.

On the other plane the lighthouse is a poetic symbol with an uncircumscribed power of suggestion. For the reader, as for Mrs Ramsay, the alternating light and shadow of the lighthouse beam symbolizes the rhythm of joy and sorrow in human life and the alternating radiance and darkness of even the most intimate human relationships:

"She looked at the steady light, the pitiless, the remorseless, which was so much her, yet so little her, which had her at its beck and call (she woke in the night and saw it bent across her bed, stroking the floor), but for all that, she thought, watching it with fascination, hypnotised, as if it were stroking with its silver fingers some sealed vessel in her brain whose bursting would flood her with delight, she had known happiness, exquisite happiness, intense happiness, and it silvered the rough waves a little more brightly, as daylight faded, and the blue went out of the sea and it rolled in waves of pure lemon which curved and swelled and broke upon the beach and the ecstasy burst in her eyes and waves of pure delight raced over the floor of her mind and she felt, It is enough! It is enough!"   [*To the Lighthouse*]

The structure of the book itself reproduces the effect of the lighthouse beam, the long flash represented by the first movement (The Window) the interval of darkness represented by the second movement (Time Passes) and the second and shorter flash by the last movement (The Lighthouse). When this aspect of the book is thought of the subject is no longer a particular group of human beings; it is life and death, joy and pain—more specifically two themes stand out, the isolation of the individual human spirit and the contrast between the disordered and fragmentary experience of living and the ideal truth or beauty to which the human mind aspires. Mr Ramsay's habit of murmuring "Some one had blundered" and "we perished each alone", which on the prose plane is a mere donnish eccentricity, in keeping with his character, on this other plane evokes the sense of chaos and of loneliness. Mr Carmichael, the remote, inscrutable old poet, addicted to drugs and unfortunate in his domestic life, is used, at the prose level, to illustrate a typical difference between Mr Ramsay, whose despotic intolerance cannot forgive his behaviour at dinner (he asks for a second helping of soup), and Mrs Ramsay's larger understanding. But Mr Carmichael has also another function. Already, in the first movement, his disinterested self-sufficiency causes Mrs Ramsay to suspect her own motives. In the last movement, while he still remains the remote, inscrutable old man (the reader never comes into direct contact with his reflections), he is also the poet who, Lily feels, shares her quest for beauty and significance.

The second movement in the book, Time Passes, has also a double function. From one point of view it is a method of recording events that mark the passage of ten years. Mrs Ramsay dies; Prue is married; Prue dies in childbed; Andrew is killed in France; Mr Carmichael publishes poems; the marriage between Paul and Minta is flawed and patched up; at intervals Mrs McNab, alone or with Mrs Bast, airs and cleans the house. Thus the years are marked and scarred, a particular ten years in which such was the history of the Ramsay family, linked with the history of England and the first European war. But, from the other point of view, it is not merely a particular ten years that is represented, but time in relation to eternity, the short span of mortal lives, contrasted with the recurring seasons and the enduring world. The pageant of the seasons is interwoven with the record of human events in such a way as to evoke the illusion of nature's sympathy, or point to the irony of nature's indifference. But in this section, brilliant though it often is, the burden is sometimes too heavy and strain reveals itself in an over-elaborate style.

A similar over-charging of the prose is felt in the descriptive interludes in *The Waves*. Their purpose is to symbolize the progress from youth to age by showing it reflected in the progress from dawn to sunset. Consequently these brief essays are not merely word-paintings of a sea-scape under the changing light of the sun, but also prose-poems evoking the changing mood and temper of mankind through the seven ages of man. Birds, insects, the objects in the house, the quality of light and sound are made to reflect the altering perceptions of man as he passes from youth to maturity and from maturity to old age. For instance, in the essay introducing that section of the book in which the characters are in the last stage of adolescence (the young men are about to enter the university, or to start their business career), the complex changes in their personality are symbolized by the behaviour of the birds at mid-morning:

"In the garden the birds that had sung erratically and spasmodically in the dawn on that tree, on that bush, now sang together in chorus, shrill and sharp; now together, as if conscious of companionship, now alone as if to the pale blue sky. They swerved, all in one flight, when the black cat moved among the bushes, when the cook threw cinders on the ash heap and startled them. Fear was in their song, and apprehension of pain, and joy to be snatched quickly now at this instant. Also they sang emulously in the clear morning air, swerving high over the elm tree, singing together as they chased each other, escaping, pursuing, pecking each other as they turned high in the air. And then tiring of pursuit and flight, lovelily they came descending, delicately declining, dropped down and sat silent on the tree, on the wall, with their bright eyes glancing, and their heads turned this way, that way; aware, awake; intensely conscious of one thing, one object in particular."

[The Waves]

Skilfully the flight and song of the birds has been made to echo the habits of young human beings, uniting in companies, rejoicing in solitude, driven together by fear of a hostile world, competitive yet co-operative, alert yet narrow in vision. But the parallel is over-ingenious; the reader inclines to attend neither to the impressions of the morning scene, nor to the mind of youth, but to the skill of the writer. The ingenuity calls attention to itself, as in some over-elaborate metaphysical conceit, or in a dream passage from De Quincey's *Opium Eater*. For Virginia Woolf's highly wrought style combines the wit of the first "yoking together things apparently unlike" with the evocative rhythms of the second:

"Now it was that upon the rocking waters of the ocean the human face began to reveal itself; the sea appeared paved with innumerable faces, upturned to the heavens; faces imploring, wrathful, despairing; faces that surged upwards by thousands, by myriads, by generations: infinite was my agitation; my mind tossed, as it seemed, upon the billowy ocean, and weltered upon the weltering waves."

"The wind rose. The waves drummed on the shore, like turbaned warriors, like turbaned men with poisoned assegais who, whirling their arms on high, advance upon the feeding flocks, the white sheep."

The first paragraph is by De Quincey, deliberately reproducing the effect of an opium dream, the second is by Virginia Woolf.

There is another reason why the interludes in *The Waves* and the central movement in *To the Lighthouse* are not wholly satisfactory. Inevitably they interrupt the mood of the narrative, they force the reader to abandon one point of view and adopt another and consequently they disturb his "willing suspension of disbelief". When the magic of a fiction works for the reader, he lives in the world the writer creates, "the mariner has his will". Any change of approach which reminds him of the art of the story-teller breaks the illusion. The structure of *To the Lighthouse* is so planned that the time interlude is unavoidable. By some means the passage of ten years must be felt—the consequent re-adjustment of the reader's point of view, his removal to a further distance from the scene of action, so that he observes the characters as tiny, featureless beings whirled about by the winds of chance, is accepted as an inconvenience necessary to the total effect. The necessity of the prose poems in *The Waves* is more doubtful. A simpler device would have been adequate to mark the passage of the years which is in any case implicit in the body of the book.

In *Mrs Dalloway* and *To the Lighthouse* the concentration necessary for the full effect of Virginia Woolf's mode of presentation is achieved by limiting the time covered by the action, as well as by restricting the number of foreground characters. In *The Waves* the span of time covered by the action is from youth to age in one generation. The reader shares the experience of that generation by direct and intimate observation of the thoughts and feelings of three women and three men. The degree of intimacy achieved, the depths to which human consciousness is explored and the wide relevance to universal human experience necessitates and compensates for this narrowing of attention. Some part of Virginia Woolf's vision of life is sacrificed and will be found again in her two subsequent books. There is less comedy in *The Waves* than in any other of her books and less of the surface of human behaviour. The form of the book allows less variation in pitch than elsewhere, there is no relaxation, and, unless the reader's attention is continually on the stretch, he may fail to notice some such event as a birth, a marriage, a love alliance, or a death which is referred to in meditation and, although submerged beneath the continual flow of life's current, is yet essential to the gradual forming and fixing of personality as well as to the impression of life created by the whole composition. Furthermore unless he gives continually that heightened attention which poetry, but not fiction, normally demands he will not respond adequately to the recurrent images and symbols upon which that impression largely depends. The reward for such vigilant reading is the depth, truth and compassion with which human consciousness is presented. It is true that the six through whom that consciousness is conveyed are in some ways alike and are in some ways exceptional. Each of them is capable of full self-development and, therefore, of that rare integrity which can attain self-knowledge. Each is capable of a sensitive and finely distinguishing response to the experience of living. In this sense they are above the average man or woman in a way comparable to that in which the tragic hero is above the normal stature. Moreover, the six are modern men and women of the upper middle class, so that their peculiar endowment with the powers of perception and of self-realization demands "a willing suspension of disbelief" such as is unquestioningly given when an audience accepts the extraordinary command of poetic language possessed by any Shakespearian character. The language in which the six express themselves even in early youth is a convention without which the writer could not communicate her vision. For instance, the children are doing their lessons and each feels the moment in accordance with his or her own temperament; no child's language could convey what they feel, but the language in the book conveys the feelings of the children, each with that singularity of attitude which will govern their whole life:

"'Those are yellow words, those are fiery words', said Jinny. 'I should like a fiery dress, a yellow dress, a fulvous dress to wear in the evening.'

"'Each tense', said Neville, 'means differently. There is an order in this world; there are distinctions, there are differences in this world, upon whose verge I step. For this is only a beginning.'

"'Now Miss Hudson', said Rhoda, 'has shut the book. Now the terror is beginning. Now taking her lump of chalk she draws figures, six, seven, eight, and then a cross and then a line on the blackboard. What is the answer? The others look; they look with understanding. Louis writes; Susan writes; Neville writes; Jinny writes; even Bernard has now begun to write. But I cannot write. I see only figures. The others are handing in their answers, one by one. Now it is my turn. But I have no answer. The others are allowed to go. They slam the door. Miss Hudson goes. I am left alone to find an answer. The figures mean nothing now. Meaning has gone. The clock ticks. The two hands are convoys marching through a desert. The black bars on the clock face are green oases. The long hand has marched ahead to find water. The other painfully stumbles among hot stones in the desert. It will die in the desert. The kitchen door slams. Wild dogs bark far away. Look, the loop of the figure is beginning to fill with time; it holds the world in it. I begin to draw a figure and the world is looped in it, and I myself am outside the loop; which I now join—so—and seal up, and make entire. The world is entire, and I am outside of it, crying, 'Oh save me, from being blown for ever outside the loop of time!'"

[*The Waves*]

In the first movement of the book, where the six are children, the characteristic music of each is first sounded. In a sense the form is simple while in another it is complex and elaborate. The interrelated themes, the subtle record of sense perceptions, emotions and thoughts, move within a simple formal design. The six are assembled together at their first school; then the group divides in two, the girls at one boarding school, the boys at another, later we see them singly or in pairs, and twice all six are brought together again. Percival, that shadowy, symbolic figure, the athletic boy and man of action, provides a centre to which the six converge. They meet for his farewell party before he goes to India, then again, years after his death, when all are conscious of the loss. As the years accumulate the characteristic music of each becomes fuller and clearer. Each separates from the others and lives an individual life. The design resembles some classical ballet in which from time to time the dancers come forward singly or in pairs and at times all combine in a concerted movement, while the spectator remains conscious of the characteristic steps of each. The analogy of the dance may serve to indicate the outer structure of the book; for its inner form a better analogy would be a sequence of odes, for the sequent monologues are far richer and more complex in their effect than any dance steps. They convey a developing vision of life seen through six pairs of eyes and together achieving a balanced picture. The six temperaments complement one another: Jinny's love of life is the complement of Rhoda's loathing and dread of it; Jinny's impulse to enjoy variety, to taste all the sweets of life and bind herself to none, is the counterpart of Susan's need to strike roots and to possess. Bernard's roving intelligence and unconfined imaginative sympathy is the complement of Neville's desire for an ordered completeness, his passion for a limited perfection, while Neville's pursuit of the intellectual life complements Louis's need to effect something in the world of affairs: "to lace the world together with our ships", and Neville's selection of the finest classical fruits of our cultural heritage complements Louis's sense that he inherits the whole history of the world:

"the long, long history that began in Egypt, in the time of the Pharaohs, when women carried red pitchers to the Nile."

Similarly, each of the six experiences the sexual impulse in a different way, expressing the nostalgia of their individual temperaments, which together compose a complete human being.

In *The Waves* one aspect of Virginia Woolf's vision of life is more completely given than in any other of her books. By narrowing the reader's attention and concentrating it upon the inner monologue of six persons, she is able to reveal, with profound insight, the experience of living. What is presented is the solitary consciousness, the reception of experience rather than its issue in action. The six combine to reveal the basic structure of human personality with its capacity for joy and pain; its earth-rootedness and its fear of life; its bondage to self and its out-reaching to others, its fragmentary perceptions and its nostalgia for perfect beauty and truth.

But, while *The Waves* brings to light one aspect of truth as the writer saw it, other aspects are thrown into the shadow. The experience of the passing of the years in a single life is fully felt, but their passing in the history of a nation is more faintly perceived. Particular scenes, school, college, a farm, a room, a London street are vividly seen reflected in the human mind. But the wider sense of place as the background for divers human activities is not felt. Six people are intimately presented, but the crowded world in which they live is almost effaced. It was perhaps the severe formality of the structure of *The Waves* and its focus narrowed on to the individual life that suggested the relaxed form and wider scope of the next book, *The Years*. In it the reader is aware of time and place in relation to the nation's life; he is aware of a social structure; he is aware of economic conditions. If *The Waves* is the nearest of all the novels to poetic drama, *The Years* is the nearest to social comedy. In the last book *Between the Acts* the two effects are beautifully combined.

CHAPTER VI

BETWEEN THE ACTS[1]

Between the Acts, though it is in some ways unlike any other of the novels, illustrates certain characteristics of the writer's vision, structure and style. Here more fully than elsewhere are combined her sense of comedy and of tragedy; her amused perception of individual idiosyncrasy and her insight into universal human feelings; her response to the given moment and the immediate sense-data and her consciousness of the historic and even prehistoric past.

In this book, after the partially unsuccessful expansiveness of *The Years*, Virginia Woolf returned to the severely disciplined form which is her special contribution to the art of the novel. It is a form which, because an apparently simple design is the vehicle of a complex experience, demands a close attention from the reader, such as is more usually accorded to poetry than to prose. As in poetry, certain effects depend upon the reader's response to sound sequences and to the multiple meanings and suggestions evoked by words and images. Other effects, however, depend, as in the traditional novel, upon character and situation.

The action is confined within twenty-four hours and takes place in one house and its surrounding estate. The central event is the historic pageant arranged to take place, on the terrace or in the barn according to the weather, as it has done annually for seven years. The main characters are the family who own the house, Mr Oliver, his son, his daughter-in-law, their two children and Mr Oliver's widowed sister Mrs Swithin, Miss La Trobe, the pageant mistress, and acquaintances who become part of the

1 The page references in this chapter are to the first edition 1941.

audience for the pageant. Minor characters include the servants of the house and the village community from the parson to the village idiot. This simple plot provides a viewpoint from which various aspects of the present are seen in relation to the past history of England. It allows also for the recurrence of certain themes which are important in the writer's vision of human life, such as the isolation of human beings, the rhythmic ebb and flow of love, the impulse to find or to create beauty order and significance.

The three main aspects of the subject are suggested by the title. At first it seems to refer only to the pageant, between the acts of which the human comedy is played. In the course of the book it becomes plain that it refers also to the interval, in which the action takes place, between the first and the second European war. The last words of the book make it clear that the title is also relevant to the emotional tension between Mr and Mrs Giles Oliver. Throughout the book there is an interval in their love. At the end they come together:

"Left alone together for the first time that day, they were silent. Alone enmity was bared; also love. Before they slept, they must fight; after they had fought, they would embrace. From that embrace another life might be born. But first they must fight, as the dog fox fights with the vixen, in the heart of darkness, in the fields of night.

"Isa let her sewing drop. The great hooded chairs had become enormous. And Giles too. And Isa too against the window. The window was all sky without colour. The house had lost its shelter. It was night before roads were made, or houses. It was the night that dwellers in caves had watched from some high place among rocks.

"Then the curtain rose. They spoke." [pp. 255-6]

The personal relations between Mr and Mrs Giles Oliver are, from one point of view, a part of the contemporary human comedy that the book presents (interwoven with stuff of another kind). It is from that point of view that we first become aware of strained relations between them. But in this final sequence the love-hate theme is played in a different key. It is associated with man as a part of nature, the human race stretching back into an indistinct past when, as Mrs Swithin has just read in her *Outline of History*, before Giles and Isa were left alone:

"Prehistoric man, half-human, half-ape, roused himself from his semi-crouching position and raised great stones." [p. 255]

It is kinship with that early forefather that causes them to fight "as the dog fox fights with the vixen, in the heart of darkness, in the fields of night". It is that union of the present with the furthest past that is evoked by the effect of the night upon the visible scene, the blotting out of all the signs of man's history. And it is the continuance of that history that is implied in the line: "From that embrace another life might be born." Such is the close of the book.

The opening is prose comedy:

"It was a summer's night and they were talking, in the big room with the windows open to the garden, about the cesspool. The county council had promised to bring water to the village, but they hadn't.

"Mrs Haines, the wife of the gentleman farmer, a goosefaced woman with eyes protruding as if they saw something to gobble in the gutter, said affectedly: 'What a subject to talk about on a night like this.'" [p. 7]

Mrs Haines is sketched in the traditional manner of outline character drawing. She is not a person we are to know intimately, her importance lies in the fact that she is the wife of the gentleman-farmer to whom Isa Oliver's love is temporarily diverted. Isa belongs to the maternal type of womanhood, whose love is directed by compassion. Therefore the wife of farmer Haines must be presented as a harsh and disagreeable creature. When Isa joins the group ("She had been sitting with her little boy who wasn't well"), the theme of her love for Haines is introduced and linked with this comical-grotesque portrait of his wife:

"What had *he* said about the cesspool; or indeed about anything? Isa wondered, inclining her head towards the gentleman farmer, Rupert Haines. She had met him at a Bazaar; and at a tennis party. He had handed her a cup and a racquet—that was all. But in his ravaged face she always felt mystery; and in his silence, passion. At the tennis party she had felt this, and at the Bazaar. Now a third time, if anything more strongly, she felt it again."   [p 9.]

The general conversation is resumed, Mrs Haines and old Mr Oliver are exchanging memories of the past; he recalls his mother, odds and ends come to the surface of the pool of memory:

"Of his mother he remembered that she was very stout; kept her tea-caddy locked; yet had given him in that very room a copy of Byron...."   [p. 9]

and that recollection calls to his mind two verses:

"'She walks in beauty like the night', he quoted.
"Then again:
"'So we'll go no more a-roving by the light of the moon.'
"Isa raised her head. The words made two rings, perfect rings, that floated them, herself and Haines, like two swans down stream. But his snow-white breast was circled with a tangle of dirty duckweed; and she too, in her webbed feet was entangled, by her husband, the stockbroker. Sitting on her three-cornered chair she swayed, with her dark pigtails hanging, and her body like a bolster in its faded dressing-gown.
"Mrs Haines was aware of the emotion circling them, excluding her. She waited as one waits for the strain of an organ to die out before leaving church. In the car going home to the

red villa in the cornfields, she would destroy it, as a thrush pecks the wings off a butterfly. Allowing ten seconds to intervene, she rose; paused; and then, as if she had heard the last strain die out, offered Mrs Giles Oliver her hand.

"But Isa, though she should have risen at the same moment that Mrs Haines rose, sat on. Mrs Haines glared at her out of goose-like eyes, gobbling, 'Please, Mrs Giles Oliver, do me the kindness to recognise my existence...' which she was forced to do, rising at last from her chair, in her faded dressing-gown, with the pigtails falling over each shoulder." [p. 10]

Such is the first statement of the Isa Oliver : Rupert Haines theme; prose comedy and poetic fantasy combine in its presentation, in the first movement or prologue of the book, in the late evening before the day of the pageant. In the first movement the historical theme is also announced:

"The old man in the arm-chair—Mr Oliver, of the Indian Civil Service, retired—said that the site they had chosen for the cesspool was, if he had heard aright, on the Roman Road. From an aeroplane, he said, you could still see, plainly marked, the scars made by the Britons; by the Romans; by the Elizabethan manor house; and by the plough, when they ploughed the hill to grow wheat in the Napoleonic wars." [p. 8]

With this theme the second movement opens. Facts are stated about the house, about the village and about the present owners of the house:

"The Olivers, who had bought the place something over a century ago, had no connection with the Warings, the Elveys, the Mannerings or the Burnets; the old families who had all intermarried, and lay in their deaths intertwisted, like the ivy roots, beneath the churchyard wall." [p. 11]

A century is but a moment in the story of the countryside. Yet Mrs Swithin's reading and reflections evoke a sense of the past which makes even the generations in the churchyard seem mere moderns:

" . . . she had stretched for her favourite reading—an *Outline of History*—and had spent the hours between three and five thinking of rhododendron forests in Piccadilly; when the entire continent, not then, she understood, divided by a channel, was all one; populated, she understood, by elephant-bodied, seal-necked, heaving, surging, slowly writhing, and, she supposed, barking monsters; the iguanodon, the mammoth, and the masto-don; from whom presumably, she thought, jerking the window open, we descend."

[p. 13]

Mrs Swithin, however, though she is the instrument to which the "prehistory" theme is mainly given is also a human personality of exquisite charm. Unlike Mrs Haines she is of intrinsic importance in the book. A few essential facts are given, as we watch her opening the curtains of her bedroom in the early morning; we learn who she is and that she lives with her brother except in winter; and we share her reflections on prehistory. Then she is presented in a sequence that combines the traditional method of introducing a character, with Virginia Woolf's own characteristic way. Mrs Swithin's thoughts, feelings and spoken words are given directly and also the impression they make on another mind. But the writer no longer confines herself to this way; she is sufficiently sure of it (as she was not in *Jacob's Room*) to blend it successfully with objective description.

The maid comes in with the morning tea and interrupts Mrs Swithin's vision of mastodons:

"It took her five seconds in actual time, in mind time ever so much longer, to separate Grace herself, with blue china on a tray, from the leather-covered grunting monster who was about, as the door opened, to demolish a whole tree in the green steaming undergrowth of the primeval forest. Naturally, she jumped, as Grace put the tray down and said: 'Good morning,

Ma'am.' 'Batty', Grace called her, as she felt on her face the divided glance that was half meant for a beast in a swamp, half for a maid in a print frock and white apron.

"'How those birds sing!' said Mrs Swithin, at a venture. The window was open now; the birds certainly were singing. An obliging thrush hopped across the lawn; a coil of pinkish rubber twisted in its beak. Tempted by the sight to continue her imaginative reconstruction of the past, Mrs Swithin paused; she was given to increasing the bounds of the moment by flights into past or future; or sidelong down corridors and alleys; but she remembered her Mother—her Mother in that very room rebuking her. 'Don't stand gaping, Lucy, or the wind'll change....' How often her mother had rebuked her in that very room—'but in a very different world', as her brother would remind her....'

[pp. 13, 14]

It is only after we have been given this direct view of Lucy Swithin, as she is in her privacy; as she thinks of herself; and as Grace sees her that she is described as an earlier novelist might have described her:

"So she sat down to morning tea, like any other old lady with a high nose, thin cheeks, a ring on her finger and the usual trappings of rather shabby but gallant old age, which included in her case a cross gleaming gold on her breast."

[p. 14]

Mrs Swithin's sense of the far past and of the near past are not only important as an aspect of her personality but also as a part of the whole composition, in which time and man's sense of time is a dominant theme. There is a pause in the music after this description and a new sequence follows which leads up to the third aspect of history; present historic time. Mr Oliver, after an interlude with his grandchildren, which is both interesting in itself and functional in the composition, opens his newspaper:

"'M. Daladier,' he read, finding his place in the column, "has been successful in pegging down the franc.'"

[p. 19]

The interlude is a comical-pathetic scene showing the author's usual insight into the child mind (shown also in *Jacob's Room*, *The Waves* and *To the Lighthouse*), and her sense of the frequent clumsiness of adults in relation to it. Mr Oliver's would-be playfulness with his grandson, whom he succeeds in terrifying, is comparable to Mr Ramsay's playfulness with his son James. The function of an episode about the children at this point in the composition (in addition to their obvious connection with the racial-continuity theme) is to lead up to Isa's second entry and the further unfolding of her character.

Isa is found meditating before her mirror in the early morning and questioning herself about her feelings for Mr Haines.

"Inside the glass, in her eyes, she saw what she had felt over night for the ravaged, the silent, the romantic gentleman farmer. 'In love', was in her eyes. But outside, on the washstand, on the dressing-table, among the silver boxes and tooth-brushes, was the other love; love for her husband, the stockbroker—'The father of my children', she added, slipping into the cliché conveniently provided by fiction. Inner love was in the eyes; outer love on the dressing-table. But what feeling was it that stirred in her now when above the looking-glass, out of doors, she saw coming across the lawn the perambulator; two nurses, and her little boy George, lagging behind." [p. 19]

Besides the light it throws on Isa's loves and her dominant maternal instinct, this scene before the mirror also reintroduces another principal theme. It was heard faintly at Isa's first entry, when the verses from Byron "formed two perfect rings". Isa is a devotee of poetry, her own thoughts tend to take shape in verse, she keeps a book, "bound like an account book" in case her husband should suspect, in which she writes her poems. In this way Isa is linked with Miss La Trobe whose pageant, besides other things, represents the endeavour to shape a work of art. But Isa interrupts her poetic meditations to telephone to the fishmonger and the sequence closes with her sorrowful reflection that, instead of looking like Sappho

"or one of the beautiful young men whose photographs adorn the weekly papers. She looked what she was: Sir Richard's daughter; and niece of the two old ladies at Wimbledon who were so proud, being O'Neils, of their descent from the Kings of Ireland."

[p. 22]

This is the close of the first movement in the composition; the main themes have been stated; the day of the pageant has been led up to; the members of the household have been introduced, with the exception of Giles Oliver, Isa's husband. The second movement opens with a scene in the library between the three adults. Further variations are played upon the time theme, the elderly brother and sister, despite their sharp difference of temperament, are bound together by their common memories while Isa, mother of the old man's grandchildren, represents the future. Then Isa looks at the books and her reflections evoke the present moment in history:

"What remedy was there for her at her age—the age of the century, thirty-nine—in books? Book-shy she was, like the rest of her generation; and gun-shy too. Yet as a person with a raging tooth runs her eye in a chemist shop over green bottles with gilt scrolls on them lest one of them may contain a cure, she considered: Keats and Shelley; Yeats and Donne. Or perhaps not a poem; a life. The life of Garibaldi. The life of Lord Palmerston. Or perhaps not a person's life; a county's. *The Antiquities of Durham; The Proceedings of the Archaeological Society of Nottingham.* Or not a life at all, but science—Eddington, Darwin, or Jeans.

None of them stopped her toothache. For her generation the newspaper was a book; and, as her father-in-law had dropped the *Times*, she took it and read...."

[p. 26]

While Isa is reflecting on what she has read (not a rumour of war, but a story of the rape of a child), Mrs Swithin enters. She is carrying a hammer; she has been making preparations for the pageant. The group is presently joined by two uninvited guests, Mrs Manresa and William Dodge; each is of intrinsic interest as a human being; each also fulfils an important function in the composition. Mrs Manresa, because she is a vulgarian and a child of nature, and as such has certain positive qualities which the more civilized lack, challenges the notion of cultural progress. William Dodge, on the other hand, like Isa and Miss La Trobe, expresses mankind's nostalgia for the beautiful, the impulse behind poetry, music and painting. Giles Oliver arrives a little after lunch has started, his train is late. Giles, besides other things, is throughout the book a principal vehicle of the sense of impending catastrophe in the modern world:

"Giles had come. He had seen the great silver plated car at the door with the initials R.M. twisted so as to look at a distance like a coronet. Visitors, he had concluded; as he drew up behind; and he had gone to his room to change. The ghost of convention rose to the surface, as a blush or a tear rises to the surface at the pressure of emotion; so the car touched his training. He must change. He had come into the dining-room looking like a cricketer, in flannels, wearing a blue coat with brass buttons; though he was enraged. Had he not read, in the morning paper, in the train, that sixteen men had been shot, others prisoned, just over there, across the gulf, in the flat land which divided them from the continent? Yet he changed. It was Aunt Lucy, waving her hand at him as he came in, who made him change. He hung his grievances on her, as one hangs a coat on a hook, instinctively. Aunt Lucy, foolish, free; always, since he had chosen, after leaving College, to take a job in the city, expressing her amazement, her amusement, at men who spent their lives, buying and selling—ploughs? glass beads was it? or stocks and shares?—to savages who wished most oddly—for were they not beautiful naked?—to dress and live like the English? A frivolous, a malignant statement hers was of a problem which, for he had no special gift, no capital, and had been furiously in love with his wife—he nodded to her across the table—had afflicted him for ten years. Given his choice, he would have chosen to farm. But he was not given his choice. So one thing led to another; and the conglomeration of things pressed you flat; held you fast, like a fish in water. So he came for the week-end, and changed." [p. 58]

This introduction of Giles Oliver presents him both as the consciousness in which the crisis of 1939 (between the acts) is most fully reflected, and also as the second principal protagonist in that interval of love, which represents part of the universal rhythm in human relations. Mrs Manresa, that "child of nature", is inevitably attracted by his manly beauty:

"He was the very type of all that Mrs Manresa adored. His hair curled; far from running away, as many chins did, his was firm; the nose straight, if short; the eyes, of course, with that hair, blue; and finally, to make the type complete, there was something fierce, untamed, in the expression which incited her, even at forty-five, to furbish up her ancient batteries.

"'He is my husband', Isabella thought, as they nodded across the bunch of many coloured flowers. 'The father of my children.' It worked, that old cliché; she felt pride; and affection; then pride again in herself, whom he had chosen. It was a shock to find, after the morning's look in the glass, and the arrow of desire shot through her last night by the gentleman farmer, how much she felt when he came in, not a dapper city gent, but a cricketer, of love; and of hate." [p. 59]

On the plane of social comedy, in this interval in the drama of married love, Giles and Mrs Manresa are drawn together, while Isa is for a time drawn towards William Dodge, who, because he worships beauty, is spiritually akin to her. He looks at the picture, not the one which is of some ancestor and provides a useful topic of conversation, but the picture of a lady, that old Mr Oliver (Bartholomew) bought because he liked it.

"'I like that picture.' That was all he could bring himself to say.

"'And you're right', said Bartholomew. 'A man—I forget his name—a man connected with some Institute, a man who goes about giving advice, gratis, to descendants like ourselves, degenerate descendants, said...said....' He paused. They all looked at the lady. But she looked over their heads, looking at nothing. She led them down green glades into the heart of silence.

"'Said it was by Sir Joshua?' Mrs Manresa broke the silence abruptly.

"'No, no', William Dodge said hastily, but under his breath.

"'Why's he afraid?' Isabella asked herself. A poor specimen he was; afraid to stick up for his own beliefs—just as she was afraid of her husband. Didn't she write her poetry in a book bound like an account book lest Giles might suspect?" [p. 62]

A little more conversation leads up to the introduction of Miss La Trobe, and so to the pageant itself. While the family wait for the pageant to begin Mrs Swithin shows the house to William Dodge, and each becomes more intimately known to the reader. The audience assemble and they consist of divers elements, of all ages, of all classes, a few newcomers like Mrs Manresa, but mainly the families who have belonged to the village for centuries. The scenes of the play, written mainly in verse and representing the periods of English history from the Middle Ages to the time of Queen Victoria, are interspersed with the comments and conversation of the beholders. The effect is that we see the modern world, both its triviality and its momentousness, against a background of the past, albeit the past conventionalized, as the average modern represents it to himself and would expect to see it presented in a village pageant. The device of the pageant, which forms the centre of the whole composition, has been so led up to and is so managed as to focus all the principal themes of the book. At the surface the reader attends to an amusing comedy of modern manners, as the villagers interpret or fail to interpret their parts, remember or forget their words, are audible or inaudible, and the audience make their comments apt or inept and always in character. Below the surface is the current of deeper meanings dependent in part on the thoughts and feelings aroused in the minds of individual members of the audience as they watch, and in part on the direct effect of the scenes on the reader's mind. Each of the principal characters is used to supply a particular angle of vision from which the pageant is seen and to reflect a particular attitude towards it. For instance, at the first pause in the action Mrs Manresa, like any other woman of her kind, baldly explains the obvious:

"'Scenes from English history', Mrs Manresa explained to Mrs Swithin. She spoke in a loud cheerful voice, as if the old lady were deaf. 'Merry England.'
"She clapped energetically.
"The singers scampered away into the bushes. The tune stopped. Chuff, chuff, chuff, the machine ticked. Mrs Manresa looked at her programme. It would take till midnight unless they skipped. Early Briton; Plantagenets; Tudors; Stuarts—she ticked them off, but probably she had forgotten a reign or two."

[p. 99]

That is Mrs Manresa's reaction to the pause in the pageant—it is a perfectly observed piece of comic characterization. Mrs Swithin, William Dodge and Isa supply each a different and a deeper note:

"'I'd no notion we looked so nice', Mrs Swithin whispered to William. Hadn't she? The children; the pilgrims; behind the pilgrims the trees, and behind them the fields—the beauty of the physical world took his breath away. Tick, tick, tick, the machine continued.
"'Marking time', said old Oliver beneath his breath.

"'Which don't exist for us', Lucy murmured. 'We've only the present.'

"'Isn't that enough?' William asked himself. Beauty—isn't that enough? But here Isa fidgeted. Her bare brown arms went nervously to her head. She half turned in her seat.

"'No, not for us, who've the future', she seemed to say. The future disturbing our present. Who was she looking for? William, turning, following her eyes, saw only a man in grey."

[pp. 100, 101]

But Isa has seen farmer Haines. In addition to this function of eliciting from each character, as it were, their own particular music, the pageant also represents the creative effort of the writer herself, in much the same way as Lily's picture represents it in *To the Lighthouse*. From this point of view the audience represent the reader in his endeavour to apprehend the significance of the whole, or in his obtuseness to it. For instance Isa's reflections on the Elizabethan play, which forms part of a scene in the pageant, is not only her own characteristic response, but is relevant also to the book and to Virginia Woolf's own conception of the writer's vision:

"Did the plot matter? She shifted and looked over her right shoulder. The plot was only there to beget emotion. There were only two emotions: love; and hate. There was no need to puzzle out the plot. Perhaps Miss La Trobe meant that when she cut this knot in the centre?

"Don't bother about the plot: the plot's nothing." [p. 109]

At the end of the scene Isa is watching, an old beldame dies:

"She fell back lifeless. The crowd drew away. Peace, let her pass. She to whom all's one now, summer or winter.

"Peace was the third emotion. Love. Hate. Peace. Three emotions made the ply of human life. Now the priest, whose cotton wool moustache confused his utterance, stepped forward and pronounced benediction.

125

From the distaff of life's tangled skein unloose her hands
(They unloosed her hands)
Of her frailty let nothing now remembered be.
Call for the robin redbreast and the wren.
And roses fall your crimson pall.
(Petals were strewn from wicker baskets)
Cover the corpse. Sleep well.
(They covered the corpse)
On you, fair Sirs (he turned to the happy couple)
Let Heaven rain benediction!
Haste ere the envying sun
Night's curtain hath undone. Let music sound
And the free air of Heaven waft you to your slumber!
Lead on the dance!

[p. 111]

Thus the fantastic doggerel of the pageant echoes Isa's particular music of racial continuity. But for Miss La Trobe the pageant is a creative act:

"Hadn't she, for twenty-five minutes made them see? A vision imparted was a relief from agony...for one moment...one moment."

[p. 117]

It is an interval and they stream away for tea, variously affected and unaffected by what she had striven to create and she suffers:

"She hadn't made them see. It was a failure, another damned failure! As usual. Her vision escaped her. And turning, she strode to the actors, undressing, down in the hollow, where butterflies feasted upon swords of silver paper; where the dish cloths in the shadow made pools of yellow."

[p. 117]

Mrs Swithin, however, has seen something, and with characteristic intuition and characteristic vagueness she tries to impart to the creator her reception of the vision:

"'Oh Miss La Trobe!' she exclaimed; and stopped. Then she began again. 'Oh Miss La Trobe, I do congratulate you!'

"She hesitated. 'You've given me....' She skipped, then alighted—'Ever since I was a child I've felt....' A film fell over her eyes, shutting off the present. She tried to recall her childhood; then gave it up; and, with a little wave of her hand, as if asking Miss La Trobe to help her out, continued: 'This daily round; this going up and downstairs; this saying What am I going for? My specs? I have them on my nose....'

"She gazed at Miss La Trobe with a cloudless old-age stare. Their eyes met in a common effort to bring meaning to birth. They failed; and Mrs Swithin laying hold desperately of a fraction of her meaning, said: 'What a small part I've had to play! But you've made me feel I could have played...Cleopatra!'

"She nodded between the trembling bushes and ambled off."

[pp. 178–9]

The multiple effect of this passage is typical. It is a faithful record of a conversation that might well take place between these two women at such a moment. It is delightfully absurd. Nothing could well be more incongruous than for the pious, simple-minded, highly sensitive Mrs Swithin to choose, of all people, Cleopatra. At the same time the passage communicates something to the reader about the central subject of the book; about time; about life's fragmentariness; about human isolation; and about the power of creative art.

The next scenes in the pageant represent the Victorian age in a brilliant fantasy. In the ensuing interval the fantasy is, in a sense, continued as well as reflected in the minds of the audience:

"'Oh but it was beautiful', Mrs Lynn Jones protested. Home she meant; the lamplit room; the ruby curtains; and Papa reading aloud.

"They were rolling up the lake and uprooting the bulrushes. Real swallows were skimming over real grass. But she still saw the home.

"'It was...' she repeated, referring to the home.

"'Cheap and nasty, I call it', snapped Etty Springett, referring to the play, and shot a vicious glance at Dodge's green trousers, yellow spotted tie, and unbuttoned waistcoat.

"But Mrs Lynn Jones still saw the home. Was there, she mused, as Budge's red baize pediment was rolled off, something—not impure, that wasn't the word—but perhaps 'unhygienic' about the home? Like a bit of meat gone sour, with whiskers, as the servants called it? Or why had it perished? Time went on and on like the hands of the kitchen clock. (The machine chuffed in the bushes.) If they had met with no resistance, she mused, nothing wrong, they'd still be going round and round and round. The Home would have remained; and Papa's beard, she thought, would have grown and grown; and Mama's knitting—what did she do with all her knitting?—Change had to come, she said to herself, or there'd have been yards and yards of Papa's beard, of Mama's knitting. Nowadays her son-in-law was clean-shaven. Her daughter had a refrigerator. . . . Dear, how my mind wanders, she checked herself. What she meant was, change had to come, unless things were perfect; in which case she supposed they resisted Time. Heaven was changeless.

"'Were they like that?' Isa asked abruptly. She looked at Mrs Swithin as if she had been a dinosaur or a very diminutive mammoth. Extinct she must be, since she had lived in the reign of Queen Victoria.

"Tick, tick, tick went the machine in the bushes.

"'The Victorians', Mrs Swithin mused. 'I don't believe', she said with her odd little smile, 'that there ever were such people. Only you and me and William dressed differently.'" [pp. 201–203]

But Miss La Trobe is not content to end her pageant with the Victorians, her conception is wider than that and more alarming. Indignantly the audience see on the programme that we are to be shown "Ourselves".

"But what could she know about ourselves? The Elizabethans yes; the Victorians, perhaps; but ourselves; sitting here on a June day in 1939—it was ridiculous. 'Myself'—it was impossible. Other people, perhaps. . . Cobbet of Cobb's corner; the Major;

old Bartholomew; Mrs Swithin—them, perhaps. But she won't get me—no, not me. The audience fidgeted. Sounds of laughter came from the bushes. But nothing whatever appeared on the stage."

[p. 208]

Miss La Trobe's belief that she can show her audience themselves reflects the author's own endeavour as a novelist to create the sense of life as it is actually lived. Miss La Trobe's sense of frustration and powerlessness extends beyond the particular moment in the pageant and suggests the universal relation between the artist and his public:

"Miss La Trobe stood there with her eye on the script. 'After Vic.', she had written, 'try ten mins. of present time: swallows, cows, etc.' She wanted to expose them, as it were, to douche them with present-time reality. But something was going wrong with the experiment. 'Reality too strong', she muttered. 'Curse 'em!' She felt everything they felt. Audiences were the devil. O to write a play without an audience—*the play*. But here she was fronting her audience. Every second they were slipping the noose. Her little game had gone wrong. If only she had a back cloth to hang between the trees—to shut out cows, swallows, present time! But she had nothing. She had forbidden music. Grating her fingers in the bark, she damned the audience. Panic seized her. Blood seemed to pour from her shoes. This is death, death, death, she noted in the margin of her mind; when illusion fails. Unable to lift her hand, she stood facing the audience.

"And then the shower fell, sudden, profuse.

"No one had seen the cloud coming. There it was, black, swollen, on top of them. Down it poured like all the people in the world weeping. Tears. Tears. Tears.

"'O that our human pain could here have ending!' Isa murmured."

[pp. 208–210]

Miss La Trobe is relieved, nature has intervened and provided the symbol she needed to lead up to her League of Nations tableau, which immediately precedes the final audacity, when the audience are shown their individual and collective selves in mirrors. The *lachrymae rerum*, the high hopes of "our proud and angry dust", and then the grotesque actuality; so Miss La Trobe rounds off her pageant; and Mr Streatfield, the vicar, with evasive references to its meaning, gives it his blessing and asks the audience to contribute to the fund for "the illumination of our dear old Church". And the audience disperses to the music of the song that has symbolically demarcated each interval:

"*Dispersed are we*, the gramophone triumphed, yet lamented, *Dispersed are we*...."

Comments on the pageant are intermingled with comments on the European situation:

"I agree—things look worse than ever on the continent. And what's the Channel come to think of it, if they mean to invade us? The aeroplanes, I didn't like to say it, made one think.... No, I thought it much too scrappy. Take the idiot. Did she mean, so to speak, something hidden, the unconscious as they call it? But why always drag in sex.... It's true, there's a sense in which we all, I admit, are savages still. Those women with red nails. And dressing up—what's that? The old savage, I suppose.... That's the bell. Ding dong. Ding.... Rather a cracked old bell... and the mirrors! Reflecting us...I called that cruel. One feels such a fool, caught unprotected.... There's Mr Streatfield, going, I suppose to take the evening service. He'll have to hurry, or he won't have time to change.... He said she meant we all act. Yes, but whose play? Ah, that's the question! And if we're left asking questions, isn't it a failure, as a play? I must say I like to feel sure if I go to the theatre, that I've grasped the meaning.... Or was that perhaps what she meant?...Ding dong. Ding... that if we don't jump to conclusions, if you think, and I think, perhaps one day, thinking differently, we shall think the same?"

[pp. 232–3]

Gradually all the characters leave the scene and the family alone remains; Mrs Swithin is left contemplating the prehistoric past in her *Outline of History*, Isa and Giles are left with the present and with the future.

*   *   *   *   *

In its structural severity *Between the Acts* resembles a musical composition, or a poetic drama. Like these it rewards vigilant attention and increasing familiarity and yet gives immediate pleasure at a first reception. Few novels have this kind of form. In some ways *Between the Acts* is an advance upon *Mrs Dalloway*, *To the Lighthouse* or *The Waves* because, without loss of depth, it has greater width of interest and greater variety of effect than they have. It owes more to the comic spirit. All her novels include the humour that depends upon fantasy and a perception of the grotesque, but the later and more characteristic work does not elsewhere include as much of the comedy of manners. At the surface the book is predominantly about contrasted manners and values. The characters, shrewdly observed and amusingly presented, are juxtaposed so as to offset one another, the scenes are comic, at times even farcical, as often as they are moving. It is a picture of present-day English life and manners in a setting which evokes the past history of England and forebodings of the future. But the full significance of the book depends, as in all her characteristic work, upon the sequence of scenes, the juxtaposition of experiences which throw light on one another, the recurrent images or symbols and (even more here than elsewhere) the variations of rhythm.

At the heart of the book lie the ageless paradoxes: man's insatiable thirst for the ideal and his constant preoccupation with the trivial; the "dateless limit" of human history and the "brief candle" of an individual life.

CHAPTER VII

A WRITER'S DIARY[1]

In his Preface to *A Writer's Diary* Leonard Woolf explained that
the book contains extracts from a diary which his wife began to
keep in 1915, and which "gives for 27 years a record of what she
did, of the people whom she saw, and particularly of what she
thought about those people, about herself, about life, about the
books she was writing or hoped to write". He had extracted and
published only what referred to her writing and "a few passages
[which] give the reader an idea of the direct impact on her mind
of scenes and persons, i.e. the raw material of her art", and "comments upon the books she was reading". Biographers, social
historians, and indeed all of us who are interested in people, will
crave for more. But in the book we have there is abundance for
any one who is interested in the art of the novel and in Virginia
Woolf as an exponent of that art. The selected extracts bring us
into contact with the writer during the process of making each
novel, from the first moment of conception to the time when the
author contemplates the child of her brain. We are again and again
reminded of that indefatigable maker, Miss La Trobe, in *Between the
Acts*. Miss La Trobe enjoying a fleeting moment of hoped success
followed almost at once by an agonizing sense of failure. Miss La
Trobe also represents the author in her courage and her fertility
of invention. Often Virginia Woolf is meditating about her next
work even before she has finished the one in hand. Sometimes,
as at the end of her struggle with *The Waves* she does this deliberately, therapeutically, she writes:

1 The number in square brackets after each quotation refers to the page
in *A Writer's Diary* edited by Leonard Woolf (Hogarth Press, 1953).

"I must hastily provide my mind with something else, or it will again become pecking and wretched...." [p. 158]

But it is also an innate drive. The overall impression left by *A Writer's Diary* is of her compelling need to write. The diary itself is a way of relaxing from the ardours and endurances of creative art without ceasing to commune with herself in articulate prose. Criticism, biography, or the rich fantasy of *Orlando*, though much more exacting than diary-writing, are also less arduous ways than novel-making, of exercising her craft. She always returns to that maximum effort of the imagination. Thinking of *Orlando* (after the publication of *To the Lighthouse*) she writes:

"In truth I feel the need for an escapade after these serious poetic experimental books whose form is always so closely considered. I want to kick up my heels and be off. I want to embody all those innumerable little ideas and tiny stories which flash into my mind at all seasons. I think this will be great fun to write; and it will rest my head before starting the very serious, mystical poetical work which I want to come next." [p. 105]

The "mystical poetical work" was to be *The Waves*.

Virginia Woolf gives an account of its making when she has completed her final corrections, on Tuesday, 14 July 1931:

"I began it, seriously, about September 10th 1929.
I finished the first version on April 10th 1930.
I began the second version on May 1st 1930,
I finished the second version on February 7th 1931.
I began to correct the second version on May 1st 1931,
Finished 22nd June 1931,
I began to correct the typescript on 25th June 1931.
Shall finish (I hope) 18th July 1931.
Then remain only the proofs." [p. 172]

That laconic outline is filled in for the reader of *A Writer's Diary* by entries dispersed throughout the two years of creative endeavour. But the story begins further back, 7 November 1928. On that day Virginia Woolf was thinking about the books she had published and about what her friends or the reviewers thought of them and what she herself thinks. In this context she writes that one reviewer found her style in *To the Lighthouse* too fluent, and she asks herself:

"Shall I now check and consolidate, more in the *Dalloway* and *Jacob's Room* style?

I rather think the upshot will be books that relieve other books: a variety of styles and subjects: for after all, that is my temperament, I think, to be very little persuaded of the truth of anything— what I say, what people say—always to follow, blindly, instinctively with a sense of leaping over a precipice—the call of— the call of—now, if I write *The Moths* [her first title for *The Waves*] I must come to terms with these mystical feelings." [p. 137]

She hoped that *The Moths*, when it was finished, would convey the sense of a reality apprehended as existing behind the veil of phenomena, that glimpse of harmony, beauty and significance which she had already portrayed as part of the experience of certain characters. *The Moths* was to be a lyrical work, expressing the content of consciousness. She hoped that it would convey this experience which eludes description or definition. There are places in the diary where she tries to express her own moments of "mystical" experience, but she can convey only that they are vivid, strange, and that they bring a sense of peace, often immediately after a despairing sense that nothing has meaning. Of the four entries in *A Writer's Diary* concerning such experience two belong to the period in which *The Waves* was developing. The fullest of these is on 10 September 1928, almost a month before the first unmistakable reference to that novel. She writes of:

"Experiences I have had here in some Augusts; and got then to a consciousness of what I call 'reality': a thing I see before me:

something abstract, but residing in the downs or sky; beside which nothing matters; in which I shall rest and continue to exist. Reality I call it. And I fancy sometimes this is the most necessary thing to me: that which I seek. But who knows—once one takes a pen and writes? How difficult not to go making 'reality' this and that, whereas it is one thing." [p. 132]

The next entry concerning *The Waves*, after 7 November 1928, is about form and is written on 28 November. She is still quite vague as to how the form will be achieved, but she expresses a determination to:

"eliminate all waste, deadness, superfluity: to give the moment whole; whatever it includes. Say that the moment is a combination of thought; sensation; the voice of the sea. Waste, deadness, come from the inclusion of things that don't belong to the moment; this appalling narrative business of the realist: getting on from lunch to dinner: it is false, unreal, merely conventional."

All this she means to eliminate from *The Moths* but:

"It must include nonsense, fact, sordity: but made transparent."
[p. 139]

In the upshot she invented a form which eliminated description of events, people or objects; the reader is aware of all these only in so far as they are reflected in the consciousness of one or more of the six characters.

The next entry about the book is seven months later, but the problem how to shape it has not yet been solved. At this stage the centre of consciousness was to be a woman without a name:

"I don't want a Lavinia or a Penelope, I want 'she'. But that becomes arty, Liberty greenery yallery somehow: symbolic in loose robes. Of course I can make her think backwards and forwards; I can tell stories. But that's not it. Also I shall do away with exact place and time. Anything may be out of the window— a ship—a desert—London." [p. 143]

Not much was to remain of this, but it indicates the direction in which her conception of the form was evolving. Three weeks later we find that she has made a leap forward towards the novel as we know it. If it was a gradual stepping and not a leap the steps are not recorded in the *Diary*. Suddenly the book we know begins to emerge on 23 June 1929:

"I think it will begin like this: dawn; the shells on a beach; I don't know—voices of cock and nightingale; and then all the children at a long table—lessons. The beginning. Well, all sorts of characters are to be there." [p. 144]

So far the resemblance to the final version of the beginning is very close. In the extract Virginia Woolf goes on to say:

"Then the person who is at the table can call out any one of them at any moment; and build up by that person the mood, tell a story; for instance about dogs or nurses; or some adventure of a child's kind; all to be very Arabian Nights; and so on: this shall be childhood; but it must not be *my* childhood; and boats on the pond; the sense of children; unreality; things oddly proportioned. Then another person or figure must be selected. The unreal world must be round all this—the phantom waves. The Moth must come in; the beautiful single moth. Could one not get the waves to be heard all through? Or the farmyard noises? Some odd irrelevant noises. She might have a book—one book to read in, another to write in—old letters. Early morning light—but this need not be insisted on; because there must be great freedom from 'reality'. Yet everything must have relevance." [p. 144]

It is fascinating to compare this with the finished novel in which, I believe, nothing of her intention was lost, but much of the envisaged means of presentation was changed. Neither the lady (as chorus or narrator) nor the moths remain. The invention of continuous internal monologue obviates the need of the nameless lady. The prose-poem intersections take over part of the function of the moths. The sense of childhood experience is achieved, both in its undifferentiated character, "not *my* childhood", and as a means of defining separate personalities: "all sorts of characters are to be there". The "unreal waves" and the "farmhouse noises", exist severally in the finished work, partly in the intersections, partly in experience registered in the monologues.

In this entry we see the original conception of the form and title of the work, in process of changing into a new conception, which will suggest the new title, *The Waves*. It was nearly three months later that Virginia Woolf realized that she would have to abandon the moths, which had been from the start her central symbol. On Monday, 10 September 1929 she wrote:

"Six weeks in bed now would make a masterpiece of *Moths*. But that won't be the name. Moths, I suddenly remember, don't fly by day. And there can't be a lighted candle. Altogether, the shape of the book wants considering—and with time I could do it." [p. 146]

The old and the new conception of form have this in common that they are a means of communicating the experience of living while eliminating consequential narrative. In this book she is aiming at maximum attention to inner experience (what life feels like), with minimum attention to external fact. Writing for herself in the *Diary*, she uses the word *reality* in two different senses (each warranted by the word's history). Sometimes it means an apprehended significance that eludes definition and cannot be accounted for in terms of sense perception or logical reasoning. At other times the word means objects and facts, as when she writes that in this novel: "There must be freedom from reality", here she clearly means freedom from the narration of facts and the description of objects. Possibly the moths were to symbolize moments of vision (reality in the first sense), possibly they were to symbolize continuity of a life outside human lives and indifferent to them, almost certainly they were also to be a technical device for marking transitions from scene to scene. Ultimately the waves, as part of the description of the day from dawn to dark, took over the second and third functions. The mystical experience, in the finished novel, is represented within the consciousness of one or other of the six characters.

A fortnight later, 25 September, she has made another start and writes:

"several problems cry out at once to be solved. Who thinks it? And am I outside the thinker? One wants some device which is not a trick." [p. 146]

On 2 November she is still uncertain how to set her characters against a background of the continuous rhythm of nature. She has not yet discovered either the "device" of internal monologues whereby the characters express themselves in turn, each recording their own life-experience, nor the "device" of the intersectional prose-poems evoking the continuity of external nature. She records:

"I am in an odd state; feel a cleavage; here's my interesting thing; and there is no quite solid table on which to put it. It might come in a flash, on re-reading—some solvent. I am convinced that I am right to seek for a station whence I can set my people against time and the sea—but Lord, the difficulty of digging oneself in there, with conviction. Yesterday I had conviction; it has gone today."

[p. 149]

By 17 March the following year, 1930, she must I think have arrived at the solution of interior monologues. She writes:

"The test of a book (to a writer) is if it makes a space in which, quite naturally, you can say what you want to say. As this morning I could say what Rhoda said. This proves that the book itself is alive: because it has not crushed the thing I wanted to say, but allowed me to slip it in, without any compression or alteration." [p. 156]

Although we do not know to what passage in Rhoda's self-recording this refers, it almost certainly points to a confidence that the author has been able, as she hoped, to "come to terms" with her "mystical experiences". Rhoda represents what might be called the negative aspect of this experience. She fears life; she feels alien from other people, she feels that the world is cruel and she apprehends an harmonious order which would contrast with the horror and muddle of human living. Bernard speaks of her, in the final monologue as "always so furtive, always with fear in her eyes, always seeking some pillar in the desert, to find which she had gone; she had killed herself".

Contiguous with the extract about Rhoda in *A Writer's Diary* is an entry for 28 March in which Virginia Woolf records one of her rare moments, as artist, of confidence. She felt she had given birth to the book, after being so long in labour.

"Yes, but this book is a very queer business. I had a day of intoxication when I said 'Children are nothing to this': when I sat surveying the whole book complete...felt the pressure of the form—the splendour, the greatness—as perhaps I have never felt them. But I shan't race it off in intoxication. I keep pegging away; and find it the most complex and difficult of all my books."

But she had not yet decided on that final monologue of Bernard's, which was to draw together all the threads in the pattern:

"How to end, save by a tremendous discussion, in which every life shall have its voice—a mosaic—I do not know. The difficulty is that it is all at high pressure. I have not yet mastered the speaking voice. Yet I think something is there; and I propose to go on pegging it down, arduously, and then re-write, reading much of it aloud, like poetry." [p. 156]

Twelve days later, 9 April, she reflects about the way the characters are presented, justifiably congratulating herself, and she contemplates the possible ill effects on the whole novel of the impending revision:

"What I now think [about *The Waves*] is that I can give in a very few strokes the essentials of a person's character. It should be done boldly, almost as caricature. I have yesterday entered what may be the last lap. Like every piece of the book it goes by fits and starts. I never get away with it; but am tugged back. I hope this makes for solidity; and must look to my sentences. The abandonment of *Orlando* and *Lighthouse* is much checked by the extreme difficulty of the form—as it was in *Jacob's Room*. I think this is the furthest development so far; but of course it may miss fire somewhere. I think I have kept stoically to the original conception. What I fear is that the re-writing will have to be so drastic that I may entirely muddle it somehow. It is bound to be very imperfect. But I think it possible that I have got my statues against the sky."   [p. 157]

About three weeks later, 29 April, she enters in the *Diary* "I have just finished, with this very nib-full of ink, the last sentence of *The Waves*". But that was not the last sentence as we know it. Indeed, the same entry records that she suspects the structure is wrong and it is nearly four months later, during the process of revision, that she writes:

"*The Waves* is I think resolving itself (I am at page 100) into a series of dramatic soliloquies. The thing is to keep them running homogeniously in and out, in the rhythm of the waves."   [p. 159]

Revision continues for eleven more months and vital changes take place in the structure before, on 17 July 1931, she records that the work is finished. For example, the entries for 12 and 22 December 1931 refer to important decisions yet to be made. The latter is more explicit about her intention than any earlier entry, she says:

"It occurred to me last night while listening to a Beethoven quartet that I would merge all the interjected passages into Bernard's final speech and end with the words O solitude: thus making him absorb all those scenes and having no further break. This is also to show that the theme effort, effort, dominates: not the waves: and personality: and defiance: but I am not sure of the effect artistically; because the proportions may need the intervention of the waves finally so as to make a conclusion."

[p. 162]

Bernard's last words were to be, not "O solitude", but "O Death": The dominance of the "effort" theme was to be rendered by the sentence that they terminate:

"Against you I will fling myself, unvanquished and unyielding, O Death."

Immediately after this come the last words of the novel, "The waves broke on the shore", separated by spacing from Bernard's words and printed in italics, as the close of the intersections, and in this way she solved the problems she posed herself on 22 December; she let the stress fall on her major theme and she sustained the pattern of the work, not only formally, by rounding this section in the same manner as the others, but also by sustaining the idea of the continuity of nature and the transience of individual human lives.

I have followed the record of her composition of *The Waves* in detail from start to finish; the *Diary* allows us to do the same with each novel from *Mrs Dalloway* to *Between the Acts*. The *Voyage Out* was finished before she began to keep her diary. *Night and Day* is not discussed during its progress, nor does she commune with herself in the *Diary* during the making of *Jacob's Room* to anything like the same extent. It is after that that she begins to watch the process of creation with increased attention and interest. *The Waves* seems the best example to illustrate the result of this because, whether or not it is her masterpiece (critics will probably continue to differ about this), it is her most extreme and original endeavour to render the apprehension of life and death from childhood to old age. But in all her novels she strives to capture some part of the consciousness of being alive, rather than to describe environment, record events, or define characters. And, since she felt that prose fiction in traditional kinds did not lend itself to this—or not in the manner and to the extent she wanted— each of her novels was a new experiment in form.

As with *The Waves*, so with each of her experimental novels, the *Diary* communicates a sense of adventure, including the excitement, the fear and the hope of discovery or achievement that the word suggests. Even more than other novelists who have recorded the birth and growth of their works, she appears to begin without any detailed knowledge of how she will proceed. This is partly because she does not start either with an anecdote (as Henry James often does) or with a character (as Conrad did in *Lord Jim*, or as Turgenev told James that he habitually did). Neither did Virginia Woolf start her novels with an idea about politics, morals or religion which the book would illustrate. Consequently the embryo of the book about to be made could not be expressed by defining a part of the content. She knew only that it would include certain kinds or aspects of experience. *Mrs Dalloway*, for instance:

"Has branched into a book; and I adumbrate here a study of insanity and suicide; the world seen by the sane and the insane side by side—something like that."   [p. 52]

Nine months later other themes have attached themselves to the work during its progress:

"I want to give life and death, sanity and insanity; I want to criticise the social system, and to show it at work, at its most intense."   [p. 57]

The first entry about *To the Lighthouse* reveals it as the only one of her novels which began with characters:

"This is going to be fairly short; to have father's character done complete in it; and mother's; and St Ives; and childhood; and all the usual things I try to put in—life, death, etc. But the centre is father's character." [p. 76]

It was, however, "all the usual things" that would occupy her, perplex her, and finally lead to her solution, for that novel, of the problem of form. The first impulse she records towards writing *The Years* is her need for a contrast after *The Waves*, which had kept so closely to the record of inner experience:

"I find myself infinitely delighting in facts for a change, and in possession of quantities beyond counting." [p. 189]

Later she speaks of "torrents of facts" and determines to write "a poet's book next" [p. 190]. It is six months later that she makes an entry pointing more clearly to her conception of the content of *The Years* (then called *The Pargiters*) and says that she wants to give the whole of society:

"And it's to end with the press of daily normal life continuing. And there are to be millions of ideas but no preaching— history, politics, feminism, art, literature—in short a summing up of all I know, feel, laugh at, despise, like, admire, hate and so on." [p. 198]

Moreover it was to cover fifty years, from 1880 to 1930. The progress of the book is more distressing to read of than that of any of the others. The agonies of endeavour are comparable to those of George Eliot on *Romola*, the book of which she said that the writing of it

"ploughed into her more than any other book....I began it a young woman,—I finished it an old woman". [*George Eliot's Life*, J. W. Cross, vol. II, p. 352]

And in part the reason why these books cost the authors so much is the same, they were operating just beyond the area in which their genius flowered. Despite her immense labour in revising and cutting down (the first draft was 200,000 words), *The Years* is only partially successful.

But, long before her labour on *The Years* was over, the *Diary* shows that the seed of *Between the Acts* was already germinating. It had indeed lain fallow in her mind since 21 August 1934 when she recorded:

"The lesson of Here and Now [*The Years*] is that one can use all kinds of 'forms' in one book. Therefore the next might be poem, reality, comedy, play, narrative, psychology all in one. Very short. This needs thinking over...." [p. 222]

Once again the work does not start from a character, a story or a moral, but from a notion about form and about the variety of aspects of life it could include. Fourteen months later, 15 October 1935, a brief reference to a book called *The Next War* suggests that *Between the Acts* was germinating:

"Three days ago I got into wild excitement over *The Next War*. Did I say the result of the L.P. at Brighton was the breaking of the dam between me and the new book, so that I couldn't resist dashing off a chapter; stopped myself; but have all ready to develop—the form good I think—as soon as I get time?"

[p. 257] 15 October 1935

In the interim, then, the general notion of form that had occurred to her fourteen months before, had developed into a particular design and the central theme was clear in her mind, as is implied by the title *The Next War*.

And yet, two years later, on 6 August 1937, she is asking herself: "Will another novel ever swim up? If so, how?" and then she reverts to the general conception of its form, as described three years before:

"The only hint I have towards it is that it's to be dialogue: and poetry: and prose; all quite distinct. No more long closely written books." [p. 285]

In the spring of the next year, on 26 April 1938, this general conception is beginning to suggest a particular shaping which is recognizably present (although much altered) in the finished novel. At this time the title is to be *Poyntzet Hall*:

"A centre: all literature discussed in connection with real little incongruous living humour: and anything that comes into my head; but 'I' rejected: 'We' substituted: to whom at the end there shall be an invocation? 'We'...the composed of many different things...we all life, all art, all waifs and strays—a rambling capricious but somehow unified whole—the present state of my mind? And English country; and a scenic old house—and a terrace where nursemaids walk—and people passing—and a perpetual variety and change from intensity to prose, and facts—and notes: and—but eno'!" [p. 289]

All these ingredients are there in *Between the Acts* and the intention to vary the tone and to use both prose and verse was carried out. But the entry suggests that she had not yet conceived the central feature in the structure—the historical pageant which became the means of invoking "'We'...the composed of many different things".

The pageant is first mentioned more than three years later, on 23 November 1940, by which time the novel is finished, though the title is not yet found, the *Pageant* is given as a possible title alternative to *Pointz Hall*. The title *Between the Acts* was not reached until the very end, 26 February 1941, when she records: "Finished Pointz Hall, the Pageant; the play—finally *Between the Acts* this morning."

More than with any other of her novels, the impact of current events must have affected the content. If, as I think, in October

1935, the title *The Next War* refers to *Between the Acts*, it indicates that the expectation of war was prominent at the origin of the book. It is certain from the work itself and from the final title (if I have understood it rightly) that this became a major theme. During the three years of active composition the shadow of Hitler's war was growing darker and in the last year of writing the book the war itself was pressing the author hard. Some *Diary* entries from August 1938 onwards indicate what the experience just before and during the war felt like to the author:

August 17 1938. "Hitler has his million men now under arms. Is it only summer manœuvres or—? Harold broadcasting in his man of the world manner hints it may be war. That is complete ruin not only of civilisation in Europe, but of our last lap. Quentin conscripted etc. One ceases to think about it—that's all. Goes on discussing the new room, new chair, new books. What else can a gnat on a blade of grass do? I would like to write P.H.: [*Between the Acts*] and other things."   [p. 300]

The time of the action of the novel is the time of that entry, when the gap between the two wars was fast closing. While she is writing the book the war starts and on 25 May 1940 she records that:

"Rodmell burns with rumours. Are we to be bombed, evacuated? Guns shake at the windows. Hospital ships sunk. So it comes our way."   [p. 333]

Five days later she describes a hospital train carrying the wounded through Sussex. By 22 June there are: "Nightly raids in the east and south coast. 6, 3, 22 people killed nightly" [p. 337]. On 16 August the planes are overhead:

"They came very close. We lay down under the tree. The sound was like someone sawing in the air just above us. We lay flat on our faces, hands behind head. Don't close your teeth, said L. They seemed to be sawing at something stationary. Bombs shook the windows of my lodge. Will it drop I asked? If so, we shall be broken together. I thought, I think, of nothingness—flatness, my mood being flat. Some fear I suppose. Should we take Mabel to garage. Too risky to cross garden L. said. Then another came from Newhaven. Hum and saw and buzz all round us. A horse neighed in the marsh. Very sultry. Is it thunder? I said. No, guns, said L., from Ringmer, from Charleston way. Then slowly the sound lessened. Mabel in kitchen said the window shook. Air raid still on: distant planes; Leslie playing bowls. I well beaten. 'My books only gave me pain', Charlotte Brontë said. Today I agree. Very heavy, dull and damp. This must at once be cured. The all clear. 5 to 7. 144 down last night."

[pp. 342–3]

She cured the "dullness" and went on with her work on *Between the Acts*. On 17 September, their house in Mecklenburg Square was bombed:

"'We have need of all our courage' are the words that come to the surface this morning: on hearing that all our windows are broken, ceilings down, and most of our china smashed at Mecklenburg Square."

and the entry closes with:

"But I did forge ahead with P.H. all the same." [p. 352]

This experience of the war itself does not disturb the pattern of the book. That remains firmly anchored between the two wars. But the events from 1935 when the first conception is recorded to 1941 when the book was finished deepened and darkened the experience that the book communicates. It still has comedy, perhaps even more than her other novels, but the prevailing tone is sombre and threatening and there is, in the whole novel, a sense of the pathos and inadequacy of human beings.

The amazing courage and resilience that enabled Virginia Woolf to complete *Between the Acts* during that time is evident throughout the *Diary*. She always knew that the high pressure at which she worked on her novels was likely to cause a breakdown. Sometimes the *Diary* refers to this. She counted the cost, devised ways to guard against the evil, but worked on. Entries recording joy in the work or moments of elation alternate with entries recording despair or conviction of failure. When each book is finished only her husband's praise can reassure her, often only temporarily. But the drive to write another was urgent and, once she had conceived the idea of the next novel, she laboured, against whatever odds, towards its fruition. Each book seems to evolve rather than to be planned and then made. She never fully foresees the shape it will take and many aspects of its evolution go unrecorded. Only the passage of time indicates what prolonged labour intervened between conception and accomplishment.

§ § § § §

Does *A Writer's Diary* contribute anything towards the reader's appreciation of the novels—as distinct from contributing towards his admiration for the author? No biographical data or account of what happened during the shaping of a work of art has any bearing on the value of the finished work. Biography or expressed intentions can at most only indicate what the work was meant to be or to do; the critic is concerned solely with what it is. At times a biographer (or autobiographer, or diarist) can enlighten the critic about causes of failure or of partial failure. A good example of this is Professor Gordon Ray's work on Thackeray, and particularly *The Buried Life*. By showing how certain of the women characters were thought of by the author as portraits from life, Professor Ray suggests an explanation of those curious contradictions between what a particular character is shown to be (foolish, nagging, possessive, merciless, etc.) and Thackeray's adulation of these characters in his comments. In such cases the extraneous information leaves the intrinsic worth of the novels concerned unaltered; but it offers an interesting explanation of flaws in them. This is not the object, nor, I hope the effect of drawing attention to what was happening to Virginia Woolf (and around her) while she was writing *Between the Acts*. On the contrary, *Between the Acts* is remarkably free from any such flaw as might have been caused by the intrusion of current events. It moves within its fixed frame, from one summer night to the next, between the wars. The characters are aware of nothing of which they could not have been aware at that time. News items that Isa or Giles read in the newspapers were in the newspapers at that time, and they suffice to give to the one her sense that brutality is near the surface, however smooth that civilized surface may seem, and to the other his consciousness of the imminent threat of war. The structure of the novel enables the author to express what she wants to express (for instance about continuity and possible progress over against the threat of extinction, or at least of the reversal of a forward trend) and to express all this while revealing, mocking, sympathizing with the little, ordinary, personal lives that have emerged, here and now, out of the historic past. There is no wrenching of the pattern nor straining for effects that the change in events, between beginning and ending her work, might have occasioned. But the critic may nevertheless gain something from reading the *Diary* and perhaps especially from reading of the years during which this last novel was made. The gain is not concerned with evaluation but with interpretation. Any work of art can be better understood when it is set in its historical context. For readers in a new generation the war experiences recorded in the *Diary* may throw light on the tone, the feeling and the ideas that are latent in the book. To re-read *Between the Acts* after reading *A Writer's Diary* is to read it in a clearer light, to see it in sharper focus.

This is to some extent true of each of the novels, and although I have concentrated, with the others, exclusively on entries concerning the invention and shaping of the book, this certainly does not cover all the interest and value of *A Writer's Diary*. Even for a reader who is exclusively interested in Virginia Woolf as novelist, the published extracts provide an historical and biographical background much wider than my choices suggest. They indicate, for instance, the intercalation amid the works of fiction, of other works; reviews of contemporaries, critical writings about past authors, biography, feminist propaganda. And, although Leonard Woolf confined himself to extracts that relate to writing, they include also glimpses of her friends and of a way of life.

It is a measure of Virginia Woolf's success as an artist that the *Diary* does not anywhere radically change the impression made by her works thirteen years before it was published. Much can be discerned about what each novel was meant to be, but the gap between that and what it became is not wide. By reading the novels, and only by reading the novels, we can share, to the extent of our capacity, Virginia Woolf's vision of life. The *Diary* helps us to interpret that vision and to relate it to the world in which the author lived. It also provides an example of how a serious artist may conceive and fashion a work.

CHAPTER VIII

VIRGINIA WOOLF AS CRITIC

Two volumes of Virginia Woolf's critical essays were published in her lifetime and four more have been published since her death. They are composed almost entirely of essays and reviews contributed to literary journals in England and America. Much writing of this kind, even when it is good, perishes as time passes; these survive partly because they are permeated by her personality and partly because they record acute critical perceptions. As we know from *A Writer's Diary*, Virginia Woolf wrote nothing carelessly or hastily. Mr Leonard Woolf records that he sometimes found as many as eight complete revisions of a review (Preface to *The Death of the Moth*). Each of the published essays is the fruit of strenuous labour, the labour of seeking for the essential truth about the work discussed and of communicating it with precision and grace. Her literary criticism belongs to a tradition inaugurated in England by Dryden, who conversed with his reader in urbane prose, and affirmed that the business of criticism is: "to observe those excellencies which should delight a reasonable reader" (*The Author's Apology for Heroic Poetry and Poetic Licence*). In this tradition the writer presupposes a reader who enjoys talking about books. Virginia Woolf borrowed the title of her collections of essays, *The Common Reader* from Dr Johnson, who had written in his *Life of Gray*: "I rejoice to concur with the common reader; for by the common sense of readers, uncorrupted by literary prejudices, after all refinements of subtility and dogmatism of learning, must be finally decided all claim to poetical honours." In all her criticism she assumes the persona of a common reader, although in fact such readers as she was can never have been common. She could read Greek with effort and French with ease; she was well acquainted with English literature of four centuries; she kept abreast of the most interesting endeavours of her contemporaries. She could only masquerade as a common reader, and yet the impression she makes by her tone and manner is always that she is addressing her equals, as Dryden did before her, or Hazlitt, or Lamb. She never speaks from the rostrum: she is neither a scholar nor a philosopher, whose aims are to add to knowledge or to redefine critical theories. Such activities belong to a different tradition of criticism, one which Johnson himself inaugurated in England and which includes Coleridge, Matthew Arnold, T. S. Eliot and I. A. Richards. It is the tradition that has most effect upon the academic study of literature.

The keynote of Virginia Woolf's criticism is not judgement but appreciation. In each essay she searches for the positive value of some book or author. Dismissive criticism occurs very rarely, only when she is reviewing a biography by some now forgotten author, and then most of her attention is given to its maltreated subject. For the most part, though the occasion may be a book under review, she is writing of old favourites, perhaps newly edited, and is rediscovering their quality. She discusses her fore-runners or her contemporaries in the art of letters; and, if she points to their defects, it is in order to show how little these matter in comparison with the characteristic qualities. In an essay called "Personalities", reprinted in *The Moment*, she almost repudiates the activity of criticism on this account. She has been reading a criticism of Charlotte Brontë by Mrs Humphry Ward and, while admitting the justness of the censure, she demurs:

"Her very faults make a breach through which one steps into intimacy. It is the fact that one likes people in spite of their faults, and then likes the faults because they are theirs, that makes one distrust criticism, and wake, after attempting it, in horror at dead of night. It will be remembered that Charlotte Brontë made herself ridiculous when she introduced a Baroness and a footman into the pages of *Jane Eyre*. Mrs. Humphry Ward points out the absurdity of the scene.... Again, no one has written worse English than Mr. Hardy in some of his novels—cumbrous, stilted, ugly and inexpressive—yes, but at the same time so strangely expressive of something attractive to us in Mr. Hardy himself that we would not change it for the perfection of Sterne at his best."

This is the expression of a mood, but it is characteristic in its insistence on the writer's personality as the magnet that draws us to his work, and in her unwillingness to quarrel with even the defects that unmistakably belong to it.

"Do not dictate to your author, try to become him. Be his fellow worker and accomplice", is the advice she gives in an essay called "How should one read a book?" (*The Common Reader*, second series). This is the path she follows, with the advantage denied to most of us that she actually is his "fellow worker". She writes as a novelist, always conscious of her own vocation. The subjects that occur most frequently are novels and biographies. She loved poetry, quoted it constantly, was acutely sensitive to its music and emulous of the poet's command of words, and she uses the word poetry to define certain effects in prose fiction that transcend the particular character or scene. But she rarely wrote of poets in her essays. Notable exceptions are two essays on contemporary poetry, *A Letter to a Young Poet* (reprinted in *The Death of the Moth*), and *The Leaning Tower*, which originated in a paper read to the Worker's Educational Association at Brighton in 1940, and is reprinted in *The Moment*; the title describes its central symbol; she points to limitations in the poetry of her contemporaries and suggests an explanation of defects that she finds are common to them all. The symbol of the leaning tower suggests their predicament.

"Directly we feel that a tower leans we become acutely conscious that we are upon a tower. All those writers too are acutely tower conscious; conscious of their middle-class birth; of their expensive educations. Then when we come to the top of the tower how strange the view looks—not altogether upside down, but slanting, sidelong. That too is characteristic of the leaning-tower writers; they do not look any class straight in the face; they look either up, or down, or sidelong. There is no class so settled that they can explore it unconsciously."

So she finds that these poets (Day Lewis, Auden, Spender, and MacNeice, before 1939) create no characters, tend to self-pity and to anger, focus their anger on scapegoats: "some retired admiral, or spinster, or armaments' manufacturer". Then, with her usual flair for the telling quotation, she illustrates these failings. The criticisms are just and pertinent; but the essay is on the whole uncharacteristic. In general she writes only of poets she enjoys (the Elizabethans above all) and only seldom is poetry the subject of a whole essay. On this occasion the subject may have been chosen for her: she knew that these contemporary poets were unattractive—even unintelligible—to the average reader and, with a good deal of sympathy for the poets' predicament, she tries to explain why this is so.

A large number of her essays are about biographies, diaries, letters and the people who wrote them. If she reviews a biography, a diary or an edition of someone's letters, she tries first to give an impression of the time in which the writer lived. What she seeks to discover is what it may have felt like to live in the Elizabethan age, in the eighteenth century, or in the reign of Queen Victoria. Her vision of the last has usually a slight distortion, because she wrote at the time when the Victorian age was too close to be seen in perspective. Its ridiculous aspects: self-importance, self-righteousness, prudery, stuffiness, tend to dominate in her vision of it. Further back in time her proportions are more just. When she writes of Evelyn's diary, for instance, in a few pages she lights up those sharp differences between our time and his that will best prepare us to read him. There is his very different attitude to knowledge:

"To take a simple example of the difference between us—that butterfly will sit motionless on the dahlia while the gardener trundles his barrow past it, but let him flick the wings with the shadow of a rake, and off it flies, up it goes, instantly on the alert. So, we may reflect, a butterfly sees but does not hear; and here no doubt we are much on a par with Evelyn. But as for going into the house to fetch a knife and with that knife dissecting a Red Admiral's head, as Evelyn would have done, no sane person in the twentieth century would entertain such a project for a second. Individually we may know as little as Evelyn, but collectively we know so much that there is little incentive to venture on private discoveries. We seek the encyclopaedia, not the scissors; and know in two minutes not only more than was known to Evelyn in his lifetime, but that the mass of knowledge is so vast that it is scarcely worth while to possess a single crumb."

And there is also the amazing difference in sensibility.

"For Evelyn was a sober man of unusual refinement, and yet he pressed into a torture chamber as we crowd to see the lions fed."

She quotes a few lines from a horribly vivid account in his diary of what he saw there, and adds:

"Evelyn watched this to the end, and then remarked that 'the spectacle was so uncomfortable that I was not able to stay the sight of another', as we might say that the lions growl so loud and the sight of raw meat is so unpleasant that we will now visit the penguins."

[*The Common Reader*, first series, "Rambling round Evelyn"]

The extracts are chosen to stretch the imagination; while we read him we must make the effort to become Evelyn and she does not minimize the difficulty.

Perhaps it is easier to identify ourselves with Dorothy Osborne writing her letters; again it is the quality of the time that Virginia Woolf will attempt to evoke. Why, she asks herself, did the art of intimate letter writing first emerge in England in the seventeenth century?

"The conditions that made it impossible for Boswell or Horace Walpole to be born in the sixteenth century were obviously likely to fall with far heavier force upon the other sex. Besides the material difficulty—Donne's small house at Mitcham with its thin walls and crying children typifies the discomfort in which the Elizabethans lived—the woman was impeded also by her belief that writing was an act unbefitting her sex. A great lady here and there whose rank secured her the toleration and it may be the adulation of a servile circle, might write and print her writings. But the act was offensive to a woman of lower rank. 'Sure the poore woman is a little distracted, she could never bee soe ridiculous else as to venture writeing book's and in verse too', Dorothy Osborne exclaimed when the Duchess of Newcastle published one of her books. For her own part, she added, 'If I could not sleep this fortnight I should not come to that'. And the comment is the more illuminating in that it was made by a woman of great literary gift. Had she been born in 1827, Dorothy Osborne would have written novels; had she been born in 1527, she would never have written at all. But she was born in 1627, and at that date though writing books was ridiculous for a woman there was nothing unseemly in writing a letter. And so by degrees the silence is broken; we begin to hear rustlings in the undergrowth; for the first time in English literature we hear men and women talking together over the fire."

[*The Common Reader*, second series, "Dorothy
Osborne's Letters"]

The mind that conceived *Orlando* is recognizable in these evoked impressions of times past; it may be Swift, writing the *Journal to Stella* in bed by candle-light, or Geraldine Jewsbury:

"independent, courageous, absurd, writing page after page without stopping to correct, and coming out with her views upon love, morality, religion, and the relation of the sexes, whoever may be within hearing, with a cigar between her lips."

[*The Common Reader*, second series, "Geraldine and Jane"]

The reader's imagination is made to work; he is set on the road along which he must travel if he hopes to share Virginia Woolf's own enjoyment of the book she has been reading.

A majority of the essays are, as one would expect, about novels and her taste for the novels of her predecessors was wide-ranging and unprejudiced. Though she objected to some of her contemporaries for their emphasis on material facts, yet she enjoyed the factualness of Defoe. The plotting and story-telling that she rejected in her own novels beguiled her in Mrs Radcliffe, Scott or Dickens. She had a keen appetite for all sorts of good fiction—not the appetite of a glutton, but of a gourmet. So she returns to novels of the eighteenth or the nineteenth century and does not "dictate to the author" but attempts to discover what he is doing. She may begin an essay by pointing out limitations, for instance of Gissing: "Partly because he reverenced facts and had no faculty it seems (his language is meagre and unmetaphorical) for impressions, it is doubtful whether his choice of a novelist's career was a happy one." Also she notices that: "Where the great novelist flows in and out of his characters and bathes them in an element which seems to be common to us all, Gissing remains solitary, self-centred, apart." His novels are marred by egotism and self-pity, and yet, before the short essay is finished we know why Gissing's novels are worth reading: "With all his narrowness of outlook and meagreness of sensibility, Gissing is one of the extremely rare novelists who believes in the power of the mind, who makes his people think." His novels she notices:

"owe their peculiar grimness to the fact that the people who suffer most are capable of making their suffering part of a reasoned view of life. The thought endures when the feeling has gone. Their unhappiness represents something more lasting than a personal reverse; it becomes part of a view of life. Hence when we have finished one of Gissing's novels we have taken away not a character, nor an incident, but the comment of a thoughtful man upon life as life seemed to him."

[*The Common Reader*, second series, "George Gissing"]

Within the compass of a brief essay she sketches Gissing's life and character, indicates the shortcomings of his work, and points with precision to his positive achievement. She leaves her reader in the right frame of mind to begin to read the novels.

Most of the major Victorian novelists are considered in one or more of her essays. This area of our literature has been much explored since her time; it would not be surprising if her impressions seemed inadequate or erroneous in the light of so much accumulated effort. Critical discussion of the novel has developed and new facts have come to light. The Brontës' juvenilia have been discovered; Dickens' life has been fully documented; the complete correspondence of Thackeray has been published in four volumes and that of George Eliot in seven. But the fact is that the justice of Virginia Woolf's impressions remains often unimpaired. Perhaps she would have responded to the novels no differently if she had been more fully informed.

A reason why this is likely can best be seen by glancing at an essay she wrote, not about a novelist, but about the poet, Christina Rossetti. In 1930 Christina Rossetti reached her centenary; Virginia Woolf reviewed a book about her which she describes as "careful and competent". Yet she feels that something essential is missing:

"Here is the past and all its inhabitants miraculously sealed as in a magic tank; all we have to do is to look and to listen and to listen and to look and soon the little figures—for they are rather under life-size—will begin to move and to speak, and as they move we shall arrange them in all sorts of patterns of which they were ignorant, for they thought when they were alive that they could go where they liked; and as they speak we shall read into their sayings all kinds of meanings which never struck them, for they believed when they were alive that they said straight off whatever came into their heads. But once you are in a biography all is different."

She runs through some of the recorded facts with relish:

"So one might go on looking and listening for ever. There is no limit to the strangeness, amusement, and oddity of the past sealed in a tank. But just as we are wondering which cranny of this extraordinary territory to explore next, the principal figure intervenes. It is as if a fish, whose unconscious gyrations we had been watching in and out of reeds, round and round rocks, suddenly dashed at the glass and broke it. A tea-party is the occasion. For some reason Christina went to a party given by Mrs. Virtue Tebbs. What happened there is unknown—perhaps something was said in a casual, frivolous, tea-party way about poetry. At any rate, 'suddenly there uprose from a chair and paced forward into the centre of the room a little woman dressed in black, who announced solemnly "I am Christina Rossetti!", and having so said, returned to her chair'. With those words the glass is broken." [*The Common Reader*, second series, "I am Christina Rossetti"]

This is the climax of the essay and now Virginia Woolf can come to the point to which she has all the while been leading: "It is the poetry that matters."

Much as Virginia Woolf would have enjoyed Edgar Johnson's biography of Dickens, Miss Ratchford's book about the Brontës juvenilia, or a dip into the volumes of Thackeray's or of George Eliot's letters, her own direct response to each author's work would not have altered. Still writing about Christina Rossetti she says: "The only question of any interest is whether that poetry is good or bad. But this question of poetry, one might point out if only to gain time, is one of the greatest difficulty." And so she leaves the biographer and takes a look at the critics of Christina Rossetti's poetry. She quotes a rhapsodical extract from Swinburne, a learned metrical analysis of *Goblin Market* from George Saintsbury, a confession from Walter Raleigh that, though he thought Christina Rossetti "the best poet alive" he cannot find words to describe her poetry: "The only thing that Christina makes me want to do, is cry, not lecture." She concludes that, so many kinds of criticism are likely to confuse: "Better perhaps read for oneself." Her essay concludes with a brilliant impressionistic account of the qualities of the poetry which she addresses to the poet herself, after confessing that "though I know many of your poems by heart, I have not read your works from cover to cover. I have not followed your course and traced your development. I doubt indeed that you developed very much." And she introduces a few brief quotations, not chosen to illustrate all the qualities she has described, but chosen because they are likely to lead her reader to explore further.

All her critical essays communicate impressions made by particular works upon her own receptive, well-endowed, well-furnished mind. When she looks at her predecessors in the art of fiction she is solely concerned with discovering the individual quality that differentiates this novelist from any other. Generalizations about the art of fiction occur, but only incidentally. Facts about the author's life or his times are mentioned but only to enable us to read him more intelligently. Comparisons with other authors are introduced only to suggest the kind of enjoyment we may expect. For example she says of Defoe: "He belongs, indeed, to the school of the great plain writers, whose work is founded upon a knowledge of what is most persistent, though not most seductive in human nature.... He is of the school of Crabbe and of Gissing, and not merely a fellow-pupil in the same stern place of learning, but its founder and master." This conveys the kind of writing; elsewhere the differentiating aspects of Defoe's novels are suggested:

"his characters take shape and substance of their own accord, as if in despite of their author and not altogether to his liking. He never lingers or stresses any point of subtlety or pathos, but presses on imperturbably as if they came there without his knowledge." [*The Common Reader*, first series]

In an essay on Jane Austen there occur three sentences which point to the essence of her achievement:

"The wit of Jane Austen has for partner the perfection of her taste. Her fool is a fool, her snob is a snob, because he departs from the model of sanity and sense which she has in mind, and conveys to us unmistakably even while she makes us laugh. Never did any novelist make more use of an impeccable sense of human values." [*Ibid.*, "Jane Austen"]

No less clearly she evokes the utterly different quality of Charlotte Brontë (who found Jane Austen cold and insensitive).

"We read Charlotte Brontë not for exquisite observation of character—her characters are vigorous and elementary; not for comedy—hers is grim and crude; not for a philosophic view of life—hers is that of a country parson's daughter; but for her poetry. Probably that is so with all writers who have, as she has, an overpowering personality.... There is in them some untamed ferocity perpetually at war with the accepted order of things which makes them desire to create instantly rather than to observe patiently. This very ardour, rejecting half-shades and other minor impediments, wings its way past the daily conduct of ordinary people and allies itself with their more inarticulate passions."
[*The Common Reader*, first series,
"*Jane Eyre* and *Wuthering Heights*"]

I have quoted this at length to indicate what Virginia Woolf means when she applies the word "poetry" to novels; later in the same essay she says: "*Wuthering Heights* is a more difficult book to understand than *Jane Eyre*, because Emily was a greater poet than Charlotte." And, towards the end of the essay, after further differentiating between the two sisters, she says of Emily: "It is as if she could tear up all that we know human beings by, and fill these unrecognisable transparencies with such a gust of life that they transcend reality." Wrenched from their context these sentences do small justice to the total impression of each novelist's work that she creates, but they may perhaps suggest the quality of her perceptions and the range of her taste.

When she approaches her own time she thinks about the novel as a form of art still in process of development. Meredith, for instance:

"has been, it is plain, at great pains to destroy the conventional form of the novel. He makes no attempt to preserve the sober reality of Trollope and Jane Austen; he has destroyed all the usual staircases by which we have learnt to climb. And what is done so deliberately is done with a purpose. This defiance of the ordinary, these airs and graces, the formality of the dialogue with its Sirs and Madams are all there to create an atmosphere that is unlike that of daily life, to prepare the way for a new and an original sense of the human scene."

[*The Common Reader*, second series,
"The Novels of George Meredith"]

She is fully aware of Meredith's defects of style, its self-conscious posturing, its uneasiness, its cacophonies, and she is a little suspicious of his lyrical setpieces. But she returns to Meredith in various essays: she is attracted to him partly because of what is new in his work and, as her manner is, she perceives the relationship between what is amiss and what is valuable:

"We are civilized people, he seems to say, watching the comedy of human relations together. Human relations are of profound interest. Men and women are not cats and monkeys, but beings

of a larger growth and of a greater range. He imagines us capable
of disinterested curiosity in the behaviour of our kind. This is so
rare a compliment from a novelist to his reader that we are at
first bewildered and then delighted. Indeed his comic spirit is a
far more penetrating goddess than his lyrical. It is she who cuts
a clear path through the brambles of his manner; she who sur-
prises us again and again by the depth of her observations; she
who creates the dignity, the seriousness, and the vitality of
Meredith's world."   [*Ibid.*]

Virginia Woolf was also aware that Meredith's reputation was
declining and she saw the reasons for this. Nevertheless, she
thought that there was in these novels a value which would ensure
their survival and that: "This brilliant and uneasy figure has his
place with the great eccentrics rather than with the great masters.
He will be read, one may guess, by fits and starts. . . . But if English
fiction continues to be read, the novels of Meredith must inevitably rise from time to time into view; his work must inevitably
be disputed and discussed."

Henry James, Conrad and Hardy were the recognized living
masters of English fiction at the time when Virginia Woolf
published the volumes of *The Common Reader*. She pays tribute
to each of them in her essays as well as to the great Russian
masters, then recently translated into English. The younger
generation, Forster, Joyce and Lawrence were rising into prominence among the discerning; their achievement was a matter
for discussion. Virginia Woolf watched their development, sometimes with imperfect sympathy. Mr E. M. Forster was a friend
whose opinion of her own novels she greatly cared about. He
admired them but always with reservations; she also had reservations about his novels. Nevertheless she is aware of the positive
qualities of his work. She remarks on his precise notation of
material facts in the following terms:

"He sees his people much at the mercy of those conditions which change with the years. He is acutely conscious of the bicycle and of the motor car; of the public school and of the university; of the suburb and of the city. The social historian will find his books full of illuminating information."

Yet his is not the kind of interest that she deplores as "materialism" in the novels of Arnold Bennett:

"We discover as we turn the page that observation is not an end in itself; it is rather the goad, the gadfly driving Mr. Forster to provide a refuge from this misery, an escape from this meanness. Hence we arrive at that balance of forces which plays so large a part in the structure of Mr. Forster's novels. Sawston implies Italy; timidity, wildness; convention, freedom; unreality, reality. These are the villains and heroes of much of his writing."

And she notices that there is a tendency towards didacticism, that "palpable design upon us" that Keats deplored in poetry. "He believes that a novel must take sides in the human conflict." She recognizes his gifts: "an exquisite prose style, an acute sense of comedy, a power of creating characters in a few strokes which live in an atmosphere of their own; but he is at the same time highly conscious of a message". And consequently, she perceives, he will cause uneasiness to his reader as he shifts from realism to symbolism:

"What does this mean? we ask ourselves. What ought we to understand by this? And the hesitation is fatal. For we doubt both things—the real and the symbolical: Mrs. Moore, the nice old lady, and Mrs. Moore, the sybil. The conjunction of these two different realities seems to cast doubt upon them both."

[*The Death of the Moth*, "The Novels of E. M. Forster"]

This is a truth expressed by Henry James in his book about Hawthorne: "Allegory is apt to spoil two good things, a story and a moral."

Among these collections of Virginia Woolf's essays there is no account of either Joyce or Lawrence as extended as this on Mr Forster. To find out what she thought about each of these we need sometimes to notice a sentence here and there in a context in which they are not her main subject. In an essay called "Modern Fiction", in *The Common Reader*, first series, she described the area that the novel of the future would explore:

"Life is not a series of gig lamps symmetrically arranged; life is a luminous halo, a semi-transparent envelope surrounding us from the beginning of consciousness to the end. Is it not the task of the novelist to convey this varying, this unknown and uncircumscribed spirit, whatever aberration or complexity it may display, with as little mixture of the alien and external as possible?"

And she recognized that some of her contemporaries were attempting such recordings of consciousness:

"It is, at any rate, in some such fashion as this that we seek to define the quality which distinguishes the work of several young writers, among whom Mr. James Joyce is the most notable, from that of their predecessors."

This was written in April 1919. By that time Joyce had published *Dubliners* (1914) and *A Portrait of the Artist as a Young Man* (1916), and *Ulysses* was appearing in *The Little Review*. In an essay written later, also included in *The Common Reader*, first series, *Ulysses* is referred to as "A memorable catastrophe—immense in daring, terrific in disaster". ["How it strikes a contemporary."] Perhaps in this instance the immense labours of scholars and critics upon Joyce's work would have helped her to discern the formal design of what then seemed to her a chaotic work. In the same essay there is a sentence about Lawrence: "Mr. Lawrence, of course, has moments of greatness, but hours of something very different." But she reacted strongly to Lawrence's peculiar power; there is an illuminating and surprising entry in the *Diary* which shows this; the date is 2 October 1932. One cannot tell which of his novels she was reading or re-reading. From the entry itself it is clear that she had returned to his work several times:

"I am also reading D.H.L. with the usual sense of frustration: and that he and I have too much in common—the same pressure to be ourselves: so that I don't escape when I read him: am suspended: what I want is to be made free of another world. This Proust does. To me Lawrence is airless, confined: I don't want this, I go on saying. And the repetition of one idea. I don't want that either. I don't want 'a philosophy' in the least: I don't believe in other people's reading of riddles. What I enjoy (in the Letters) is the sudden visualization: the great ghost springing over the wave (of the spray in Cornwall) but I get no satisfaction from his explanations of what he sees. And then it's harrowing: this panting effort after something....Then too I don't like the strumming with two fingers—and the arrogance. After all, English has one million words: why confine yourself to 6?"

This is not, of course, criticism; Virginia Woolf in her diary is talking to and for herself. Nevertheless, even the most ardent admirer of Lawrence would probably recognize what she is pointing to. Whatever she has omitted, the obstacles she notes are there, and the force of Lawrence's writing has been felt.

When we turn from these private thoughts about Lawrence to a published essay written in 1931, the year after Lawrence's death we find that the personal feeling is under control. She points with precision to the quality and kind of Lawrence's writing. She begins by admitting to a prejudice aroused in her by the type of adulation that surrounded the figure of Lawrence at this time.

"The chants of the worshippers at the shrine of Lawrence became more rapt; their incense thicker and their gyrations more mazy and more mystic...it was the irritation roused by the devout and the shocked, and the ceremonies of the devout and the scandal of the shocked, that drove one at last to read *Sons and Lovers* in order to see whether, as so often happens, the master is not altogether different from the travesty presented by his disciples."

Then in an essay of less than four hundred words, she records her impressions. The essay is appreciative and receptive, although she had not chosen the book that a modern critic would select, it points to the central achievement in his work. First she notes the force and clarity of presentation. She says of the book:

"Here it lay, clean-cut, decisive, masterly, hard as rock, shaped, proportioned....The lucidity, the ease, the power of the writer to indicate with one stroke and then to refrain indicated a mind of great power and penetration."

She remarks on the realism of the background, the sharpness of detail and the seeming artlessness of the writing:

"One never catches Lawrence—this is one of his most remarkable qualities—'arranging'. Words, scenes flow as fast and direct as if he merely traced them with a free rapid hand on sheet after sheet. Not a sentence seems thought about twice: not a word added for its effect on the architecture of the phrase."

And yet, she notes, the reader is under the author's spell:

"The impatience, the need for getting on beyond the object before us, seem to contract, to shrivel up, to curtail scenes to their barest, to flash character simply and starkly in front of us. We must not look for more than a second; we must hurry on."

She conveys the sense of urgency and of being held in thrall by Lawrence, expectant. "But to what?" she asks are we being hurried; she perceives that it is always to one of those moments in which Lawrence's vision is most intense and powerful:

"to some scene which has very little to do with character, with story, with any of the usual resting places, eminences, and con-summations of the usual novel. The only thing that we are given to rest upon, to expand upon, to feel to the limits of our powers is some rapture of physical being. Such for instance is the scene when Paul and Miriam swing in the barn. Their bodies become incandescent, glowing, significant, as in other books a passage of emotion burns in that way. For the writer it seems the scene is possessed of a transcendental significance. Not in talk nor in story nor in death nor in love, but here as the body of the boy swings in the barn."   [*The Moment*, "Notes on D. H. Lawrence"]

Perhaps these impressions of the effect produced on Virginia Woolf when she read *Sons and Lovers* give as clear a light by which to begin to read Lawrence as could volumes of laborious exegesis.

Virginia Woolf wrote of Hazlitt:

"Even in his most perfunctory criticism of books we feel that faculty for seizing on the important and indicating the main out-line which learned critics often lose and timid critics never acquire."
[*The Common Reader*, second series, "William Hazlitt"]

Save for the inapplicable word "perfunctory", this describes her own achievement. The word is defined in the Oxford Dictionary "Merely to pass muster, or done with the least possible effort", but Virginia Woolf, even when jotting down a passing thought in her diary, felt, thought and wrote with energy. In her published work energy of exploration is matched by the artist's energy moulding the rhythm of a phrase, the structure of a sentence, the shape of a paragraph. Her individual use of language gives a personal accent to everything she wrote. Nor did she aspire to impersonal judgements; often she reminds the reader that the recorded impressions are those of a particular mind in particular circumstances. Hers was a mind of great power and of marked idiosyncrasy. She delighted in the byways of literature and in eccentric, half-forgotten writers and characters. Especially she loved to write of gifted women, the famous, but also the obscure.

Her feminism (which led to some rhetorical excesses in *Three Guineas*) was a spur to her imagination in a number of essays in which she resuscitates minor women writers whose gallant personalities deserve to outlive their works. She is attracted to these eccentric, frustrated, intelligent women because of their difficulties (lacking, as they did, "a room of one's own"), but she is also fascinated by eccentricity, whether masculine or feminine. It is personality that interests her, the oddness of human beings. So, in her critical essays, she almost always evokes an image not only of the work, but of the man or woman who made it. Behind the writing, however slight or imperfect, she sees the living author. She does not treat the work as though it were a cryptic autobiography; works and writers remain separate, but she is interested in both. When she writes her essays she is still the novelist, projecting herself into other lives and other minds, and she is still the artist whose medium is the English language. In "A Letter to a Young Poet" there is a passage about "the art of writing..."; she says that:

"The art of having at one's beck and call every word in the language, of knowing their weights, colours, sounds, associations, and thus making them, as is so necessary in English, suggest more than they can state, can be learnt of course to some extent by reading—it is impossible to read too much; but much more drastically and effectively by imagining that one is not oneself but somebody different. How can you learn to write if you write only about one single person?" [*The Death of the Moth*]

She herself was well-equipped with extensive reading and with an outgoing imagination; she was also a masterly technician. Consequently in that letter, though she sustains an illusion of informality she shapes an argument, points a moral, reveals an attitude of mind and indicates a literary principle without for a moment ceasing to entertain. Her prose has certain affinities with poetry—it is cadenced and must be heard, at least with the inward ear, and it is shot through with fantasy, humour and wit, "yoking together things apparently unlike". Nevertheless, it is prose; and, like the prose of her novels, it is flexible, various and sinuous, winding its way into and around the presented books and characters.

In her own kind of criticism Virginia Woolf is among the masters. It is not the academic kind because it is not cautious; it is not judicial, and it makes no attempt to be exhaustive. She assumes that works of art, like human beings, cannot be perfectly known. Just as, in her fiction, she does not sum up a character but shows it in various lights, so in her critical essays she implies that each work has many aspects. She lures us to read or to re-read, not to accept a verdict or to label a specimen.

INDEX

INDEX